TWAYNE'S WORLD AUTHORS SERIES

A Survey of the World's Literature

Sylvia E. Bowman, Indiana University

GENERAL EDITOR

GERMANY

Ulrich Weisstein, Indiana University

EDITOR

Martin Buber

(TWAS 269)

TWAYNE'S WORLD AUTHORS SERIES (TWAS)

The purpose of TWAS is to survey the major writers—novelists, dramatists, historians, poets, philosophers, and critics—of the nations of the world. Among the national literatures covered are those of Australia, Canada, China, Eastern Europe, France, Germany, Greece, India, Italy, Japan, Latin America, the Netherlands, New Zealand, Poland, Russia, Scandinavia, Spain, and the African nations, as well as Hebrew, Yiddish, and Latin Classical literatures. This survey is complemented by Twayne's United States Authors Series and English Authors Series.

The intent of each volume in these series is to present a critical analytical study of the works of the writer; to include biographical and historical material that may be necessary for understanding, appreciation, and critical appraisal of the writer; and to present all material in clear, concise English—but not to vitiate the scholarly content of the work by doing so.

Martin Buber

By WERNER MANHEIM

Indiana University at Fort Wayne

Twayne Publishers, Inc. :: New York

181.3
M 277

ISBN 0-8057-2182-7
MANUFACTURED IN THE UNITED STATES OF AMERICA

FOR ELIANE

". . . Denn Ewiges hört ihm und hört uns zu,
Wie wir aus ihm ertönen, ich und du."

Preface

The life of Martin Buber, seemingly complex because of his active participation in so many fields, was actually a very simple one in which he endeavored, as an individual, to lead the perfect life in a total exchange with man and society of the kind he envisioned for the future of humanity. Since, in addition to the spoken word, understanding in silence between men was the essence of the relationship he considered ideal, written expression was to him merely a necessary substitute; and, in order to elevate the role of writing in German and Hebrew, Buber attempted a language that would recreate thoughts and acts, fantasy, dreams, and the wonderment of a silence that would be similar to the vital meaning of a pause in music. In this language he had to give new substance to words abused, worn, and deteriorated in meaning.

Those who experienced the actual sound of Buber's speech are even more aware of his concern about the inadequacy of the written word which replaces spoken sound—a discrepancy which becomes even more obvious when one attempts to approach this problem in yet another language. In order to duplicate the special atmosphere created by Buber in filling old words with new meanings, or in having words evoke more than one image, it is necessary to make a similar effort in the English language. To preserve the poetic intent, it was sometimes necessary in this study to coin words that only hint at existing ones since literal translations would not quite catch the specific shading in Buber's usage. All translations appearing in the text are my own. In the case of longer passages of prose or poetry, the original is given in the Notes and References.

Despite Buber's preference and respect for the sound of words, he left a rich legacy of written works, which, for those who did not experience the overwhelming impression conveyed by his real person, are the only expression that might indicate the significance of one of the great men of our era. Buber's literary contributions range from the anecdote to analyses of the works of the world's great philosophers and poets, from questions about the role of the artist to his own concept of *I* and *Thou*, from a comparison of Judaism with Christianity and other world religions to views on a utopian state, from the poems to the epoch-making translation of the entire Old Testament from Hebrew into German, begun in collaboration with Franz Rosenzweig and completed by Buber alone in 1961, after more than thirty-five years of work.

This study attempts to show the meaning and beauty of Buber's words. Elucidation of the German Buber Bible, as well as his writings dealing with Bible exegesis, are left, however, for worthier and better qualified scholars. In order to stay within the limits of the literary approach of the series, this study will only note briefly Buber's enormous interest in applying his thought to education and to man's existence as a social and political being. In this way, the reader might become aware of the fact that Buber's writings are more than merely literary products. Above all, Buber had an immense devotion to man's future and foresaw the danger of certain political developments. Also for reasons of space, no attempt is made to furnish a strict biographical outline of Buber's life; only the events that contributed to his literary achievements are indicated.

During his long, rich life Buber dealt with the ideas, ideals, aspirations, and the reality of the phenomenon "man." Since he must be considered one of the greatest thinkers of the twentieth century, it would be presumptuous for anyone to claim to be equally well informed and critical in a discussion of all of his works. Besides, the limitations in scope imposed on Twayne's World Authors Series enforce selectivity. I will attempt to trace the gradual crystallization of Buber's concept of *I* and *Thou* and to place Buber, without categorizing him, in the context of modern man, as philosopher, religious thinker, artist, and social being.

The first chapters of my study deal with the background and the influences which helped to form Buber's unique philosophy. In subsequent chapters, the focus is on the gradual development of his dialogical principle, which finds poetic expression in three works: *Daniel, Ich und Du,* and *Zwiesprache.* Buber's life-long occupation with thoughts, expressions, and problems of Judaism, culminating in the rediscovery of the most valuable aspects of Hasidism[1] in their effect on his own ideas as a philosopher and poet are discussed in the chapter entitled "Hasidism" (a Jewish movement sanctifying the everyday life which reached its peak in eighteenth- and early nineteenth-century Poland).

It is hoped that from a discussion of some of Buber's key works dealing with his particular view of man in his double relationship to the world and God, his unique spirit and his hopes for the future of man will emerge. A historical review of those philosophers and thinkers who played a role in the development of his thinking cannot be undertaken here. However, since a general discussion might add to an understanding of Buber's intellectual aims, a few words will indicate the philosophical trend from which he derived his impetus as well as his critical stance.

The greatness of Buber's thinking and his contribution to an incredibly large number of disciplines have been treated by a number of authors, in particular by Hans Kohn, and in more recent days, by Maurice Friedman. But even though the words in Buber's world have greater suggestive power than a literal definition could convey, their beauty and their poetic value have not yet been appraised.

Without wanting to pursue an analytical discussion, the "literary" approach of this investigation is to be understood in the broadest sense: dealing with language, words, thought, and the most intimate human experience that can be dealt with in sound or writing. But, more important yet, since Buber was mainly concerned with existence itself, even his artistic greatness can only appear as a fragment of his life.

In his thinking and his attitudes, Buber reveals a position that might be characterized as being of philosophical-religious intent, in which he shuns, however, definite philosophical answers, particularly when these answers do not involve man's spiritual and physical existence. Philosophers dealing with a theory of cognition frequently insist upon their own particular concepts to such an extent that they adapt their views of real life to their thinking. Although one might be greatly interested in the results of the investigations of a Kant, a Kierkegaard, a Freud, or a Sartre about "What man is," the question itself cannot be answered. These philosophically oriented men have one point in common: they discuss only one aspect of the human endeavor—the intellectual or spiritual search. None of them includes the physical reality of human existence. In contrast to such authors, great religious personalities include all aspects of man's life and are not exclusively concerned with the metaphysical realm as is the philosopher, or the subconscious, as is the psychologist.

A religious life which is free and independent of church interpretation believes in a mutual confrontation of the divine and human spirit. In the truly religious person, neither should the divine element be overpowering by underlining the "creatureness" of man, nor should man consider himself the "measure of all things" by creating his particular kind of God, a God who, far from reality, becomes the recipient of monologues, reserved for Him on special days and at specified hours.

Because religion encompasses all spiritual aspects of God and man, Buber felt that it can succeed more than any dogmatic philosophy in getting closer to the reality of being—if religion means more than theology or any adherence to a dead dogma, as Moses, Lao-tse, Confucius, and Jesus have proved; for none of these religious leaders was concerned with a specific answer for others. When questions were asked of them, they knew that an answer could not be prescribed but only found by the individual within his chosen community.

The visual artist, the musician, and the poet closely approximate this religious approach. Their answer, given in their artistic creations, is the result of a confrontation with a divine element, of a total self-abandonment to a source beyond human endeavor to which the artist responds in the hour of inspiration. The creative act happens in constant renewal and adjustment in the remembrance of that timeless moment, that spark, or *"instant créateur"* that "sparked" artists such as Michelangelo, Rembrandt, Beethoven, and Goethe.

In his writings, Martin Buber, the artist, creates in such timeless moments: but, besides, he is trying to capture the centricity of existence itself. Man thus is responsible for his own reality and for his interrelationship with the human and the divine. Seen in this light, writing becomes an artistic compromise, because written words can only refer to the reality of lived life. Writing cannot reproduce the actual experience of the speaking or the sound of a word; but the experience, subjected to the element of time, can be captured only in the *memory* of words.

In early religions, little was written down, and believers depended mostly on verbal tradition. Lao-tse spoke in images; Buddha and Jesus, in parables. In Judaism and in its most recent manifestation, Hasidism, this oral tradition is contained in epigrams and anecdotal legends. But time abused the word, and it had to be recaptured and filled with essence. Like other poets, Buber was as much aware of the beauty and importance of the word as Rainer Maria Rilke who wrote:

> The poor words, which are hungry in daily life,
> The unpretentious words, I love them so,
> From my feasts I give them colors.
> Then they smile and grow slowly happy.[2]

This awareness of the spiritual and esthetic quality of language is part of Buber's greatness and can be witnessed in his painstaking choice of words, from his early work *Ich und Du* to his last poems. Frequently, because of the significance of his philosophy, readers have overlooked the fact that Buber valued not only *what* he said but also *how* he said it.

According to the Bible, in the beginning was the word; and Buber speaks of the word as the link between men and between man and God. A word is a world. In the compass of this very special outlook there can never be a question of the "literariness" of words, for their broad significance must include life. Thus, to Buber, the word represents a symbol of real life. Words that strive for a solution, a fusion, and a synthesis can amount only to a momentary satisfaction; for real progress comes from man's constant search and his willingness to accept life's contradictions and to recommence at any given moment his striving for truth.

Since, to Buber, written expression was only one aspect which can but substitute for the lived moment, that moment which was spoken or withheld, it was hoped that with a face-to-face meeting with Buber's person—which might also clarify some questions—an element of immediacy could be inserted into this book. But this meeting, planned long in advance, did not take place; for, on the day it was to occur in Jerusalem, in the summer of 1965, Buber left this world, which he so dearly loved. This meeting would have been a second and a different one. The first, which had an enormous influence on the lives of a group of young people, happened in the 1930's at a youth conference in Lehnitz near Berlin. The present book, although written under the impact of many years past, can thus only aim at being a stimulus but does not portray the whole person of Martin Buber, which can be measured only by those who experienced the sound of his spoken word and the wisdom of this modern *Zaddik*. It is to the memory of these unique moments that this book is dedicated.

Contents

Chronology

1878   February 8, Martin Buber born in Vienna.

1880–   Following the divorce of his parents, he is educated by his
1891   grandparents, Salomon and Adele Buber, in Lemberg (Galicia), Poland. First contacts with Ḥasidism. Lives with his father, who had remarried. Attends Polish Gymnasium in Lemberg.

1896   Studies philosophy at the University of Vienna.

1897–   Studies at the University of Leipzig.
1899   Founds Zionist organization and Association of Jewish students.

1899   Summer studies of philosophy, history of art, literature, psychiatry (under Wilhelm Wundt), and philology at the University of Zurich. Delegate at Third Zionist Congress in Basel. Summer, 1898, and fall, 1899, at the University of Berlin; studies under Wilhelm Dilthey and Georg Simmel. Marries the non-Jewish novelist, Paula Winkler, who wrote under the pseudonym "Georg Munk."

1900   Member of *Neue Gemeinschaft* (New Community), where he meets Gustav Landauer. Founds a department for Jewish art and science within the Zionist movement.

1901   Publisher of *Die Welt* (The World), a Zionist periodical.

1903–   Withdraws from the Zionist political scene after the death of
1904   Theodor Herzl. Intensive studies of the Bible, Hebrew; rediscovery of Ḥasidic writing. Interest in foreign epics and myths (Finnish *Kalevala* and Chinese tales). Doctor of Philosophy at the University of Vienna.

1905–   First publication of Ḥasidic books, written in Italy: *Die*
1906   *Geschichten des Rabbi Nachman* (1906).

1909   His important article on Tao in his edition of *Reden und Gleichnisse des Tschuang-Tse* (Speeches and Allegories of Tshuang-Tse) (1910).

1911	First publication of his speeches on Judaism in Prague, *Drei Reden über das Judentum* (Three Speeches on Judaism).
1913	Publication of *Daniel*, containing his first poetic formulation of man's duality.
1914	Acquaintance with Franz Rosenzweig, who becomes a close friend.
1916	Speaks against Jewish liberalism as proclaimed by the neo-Kantian Hermann Cohen. Founds the journal, *Der Jude* (The Jew), organ of German Jewry, which existed until 1924. First draft of *Ich und Du* (I and Thou).
1919–1921	Member of *Hapoël Hazaïr*, an organization wanting a revolutionary colonization of Palestine.
1921	Withdraws from Zionist work.
1922	Publication of *Ich und Du.*
1923	Professor at *Freies Jüdisches Lehrhaus* (free institute of Jewish adult education) in Frankfurt am Main, until 1933. Also appointed honorary professor of religious science at the University of Frankfurt.
1925	Begins translation of Bible with Franz Rosenzweig. Founds *Jüdischer Verlag* (Jewish Publishing House). Helps found *B'rith Shalom*, an organization advocating peaceful coexistence of Arabs and Jews.
1926	Publishes *Die Kreatur* with the Catholic theologian Joseph Wittig and the Protestant psychiatrist Viktor von Weizsäcker.
1927	First visit to Palestine.
1929	Franz Rosenzweig dies after a long illness.
1932	Publication of *Königtum Gottes* (Kingdom of God), important Bible interpretation, in which he incorporates ideas of the religious sociologist, Max Weber, whom he greatly admired.
1933	Dismissal from the University of Frankfurt.
1933–1938	Lives in Heppenheim an der Bergstraße, writing and helping and encouraging German Jewry. Leaves for Palestine. Appointed as a professor of social philosophy, Hebrew University, Jerusalem.
1943	Publication, in Hebrew, of his only novel, *Gog and Magog* (English translation, 1945, as *For the Sake of Heaven*). The German version, *Gog und Magog*, was first published in 1949.
1949	Director of teachers' training, designed to teach newcomers to Israel.

1951   Visits the United States. Lectures at American universities. Receives the Hanseatic Goethe prize.

1953   Receives the peace prize of the German book trade.

1957   Speaks at the eightieth anniversary celebration of his friend, the Nobel Prize winner, Hermann Hesse.

1958   His wife dies.

1961   Edits his wife's stories, under the title, *Geister und Menschen* (Ghosts and Men). Completes the German translation of the Old Testament after thirty-six years of work.

1962   Writes introduction to the collected works of Richard Beer-Hofmann.

1963   Receives the Erasmus Prize.

1965   June 13, dies in Jerusalem.

CHAPTER 1

Formative Years and Years of Decision

I. *Early Life and Student Years*

BORN in Vienna in 1878, Martin Buber in early childhood came to Lemberg, the capital of Galicia, where the variety of spoken languages left a deep mark on him. German was the language spoken in the home of his parents and grandparents; Polish in street and school, Yiddish in the Jewish quarters, and Hebrew in the synagogue. His grandparents had a great influence on his development. The grandmother, Adele Buber, who educated him until his fourteenth year, brought him under the spell of German language and literature, which had enhanced her younger years in the dreary world of the ghetto, and she instilled in her children and grandchildren her love for the German Romantics, such as Jean-Paul and E. T. A. Hoffmann. The grandfather, Salomon Buber, a representative of the Haskala, the Jewish movement of enlightenment, was the leader of a new bourgeois Jewry in Lemberg. A master of the Hebrew language, he was a famous editor of Midrash texts (early Bible commentaries).

In Galicia, Martin Buber had his first contact with the Eastern Jewish movement of Ḥasidism (see chapter 6), and although this new form of lived religion and genuine human community was already in its decline, it had a lasting influence on the youth. And in later years, after a period of intellectual freedom, he returned to those teachings, never to give them up again.

At the age of eighteen, Buber enrolled at the University of Vienna. In this city, he was strongly influenced by the theater. He now heard the German language as it was spoken on the stage. What had been only "signs" in books he heard now as "sound." He began to love this language and the people who spoke it, for their lightheartedness enchanted Buber and permeated his speaking and writing; even when he later detached himself from what he considered the "playful Romanticism" of some poets of the Austrian school, such as Hugo von

Hofmannsthal, Richard Beer-Hofmann, and Arthur Schnitzler, he retained the softness and emotionality of language characteristic of the Viennese people and their theater. These first encounters with language were the beginning of Buber's respect for the inner meaning of words. The word, beyond its interpretation, began to represent to him a vital aspect of an individual human utterance and a symbol of communication between man and his fellow man and between man and God.

Like other figures of literary Vienna at the turn of the century, Buber came under the influence of Friedrich Nietzsche and Søren Kierkegaard; but he also admired writers of a specifically Jewish literature—whether written in Hebrew, Yiddish, or German—Micah Berdyczevski and Isaac Perez and their attempt to revitalize Hasidism, Simon Dubnov and his critical view of the role of the Jews in history, and Theodor Herzl and his Zionism (the modern way of Jewish life culminating in the establishment of a Jewish state as a political unit). These were undercurrents in Buber's student years, but his real interest lay in philosophy, and he showed a particular preference for the beauty of language and thought exhibited by Jacob Böhme, the German medieval mystic.

While in Vienna, Buber had close contact with Gustav Landauer and his circle, the *Neue Gemeinschaft* (New Community). He read Landauer's modern version of the speeches of Meister Eckhart, which retained the simplicity of their medieval spirit largely because of Landauer's revaluation of the words whose meaning had disintegrated in the modern language. This new approach to the art of translation greatly influenced Buber in the years to come and culminated in his interpretative German translation of the Hebrew text of the Old Testament.

In the Landauer circle, whose slogan was "against the bourgeoisie of the mind," Buber was exposed to many discussions and theories about the role of art in society and history. Despite the members' stress on their elite position in society—an attitude rather foreign to Buber—some of their ideas deeply impressed him; and he was to incorporate similar thoughts in his own principles. For example, in Landauer's view, art was created for the educated upper classes by a few privileged persons. The individual artist, who lives in a melancholy yet unwanted isolation, is aware of the discrepancy between individual experience and the uncomprehending masses who have, for centuries, been reared to hate him as a member of a group with greater intellectual resources than their own. To the member of this circle, history, throughout the ages, had indirectly favored the privileged few who determined the culture of their respective country. The Landauer circle—and Buber with it—felt that the historic hour for a cultural renewal had come at the turn of the century and had brought about a Renaissance of Jewish literature that showed an influence of contemporary German writing emanating from literary personalities such as Gerhart Hauptmann, Hugo von Hofmannsthal, and Rainer Maria Rilke.

II   *Under the Spell of Zionism and Ḥasidism*

Men like Buber wanted to build Zionism on a cultural basis so that it would be more than a philanthropic movement. In 1900, Buber founded a section for Jewish art and science within the Berlin Zionist organization. He even thought of founding a Jewish stage in Vienna, such as existed in Prague. Curiously enough, despite these artistic aspirations, he became editor of *Die Welt* (The World), a politically oriented magazine and party organ founded by Herzl.

From the beginning, Buber's interpretation of Zionism differed from that of Herzl. Herzl wanted a political state that could compete with all other nations, whereas Buber wanted to re-create the biblical state and fulfill the destiny of the Jews. In contrast to Herzl's political Zionism, Buber's represents a cultural strain within Judaism, an elaboration of its spiritual heritage. In this spirit, Buber founded the Jüdische Verlag (Jewish Publishing House), which sought to encourage Jewish art, literature, and science. He also edited *Jüdische Künstler* (Jewish Artists), a journal honoring artists like Joseph Israels, Max Liebermann, Lesser Ury, and Jacob Epstein. But of greatest interest to Buber was poetic writing, and he helped introduce the legends of Ḥasidism and the works of Achad-Haam (the Ukrainian-born Jewish author who wrote in Hebrew and, like Buber, advocated cultural Zionism) to the German-speaking public.

During these years, Buber's views on Zionism departed greatly from those of the recognized Zionist leaders. To him, Herzl's and Max Nordau's projected state in Palestine was devoid of all vitality. To Buber, a settlement of Jews could only become organic in contact with a spiritual-historical consciousness which seemed to exist in Eastern Europe, where the enthusiasm for Zion expressed itself in a newly awakened Hebrew literature under the leadership of Isaac Perez, teller of symbolic anecdotes, and the lyric poet Chaim Bialik.

Herzl's misunderstanding of Buber's outlook, which led to a rift between the two men, did not keep Buber from retaining his admiration for Herzl's immense organizational strength and for the enthusiasm he had inspired in his followers, attributes important for the future of a Jewish state. After Herzl's death in 1910, Buber was instrumental in making Zionism a real part of an active Jewish Renaissance movement.

Zionism meant to Buber the battle for inner liberation; and, as the years went by, he became ever more opposed to power politics. He did not believe in Zionism as an escape, as a means to improve the situation of world Jewry, but as the new formulation of a people's community. To Buber, Zionism was not an answer to anti-Semitism but the renewal of historical Judaic traditions, the obligation to insure their continuity in the land of Palestine, and the hope that this ideology was also to form part of a general European cultural movement. He believed that real nationalism is not based on the belief in the difference of peoples, but that in stressing individual qualities in each, such nationalism helps broaden the views of man and ultimately brings about a deeper understanding among societies. Thus, nationalism complements humanity. Herzl's Zionism was leaning toward the future, because he felt that the present was a vacuum for Judaism which he was not interested in filling, whereas Buber's was focused on the present, and as early as 1917, he hinted at a new form of human coexistence when he said: "Zionism must speak to the community of all peoples."[1]

Another important influence on Buber was Ḥasidism, which represented to him a new religious force in an age that was yearning for the spiritual permeation of existence. Buber, like many a writer and philosopher during the nineteenth century, was striving for spiritual purification and penetration, and he was seeking clarification in his intense studies of Ḥasidism, of Oriental teachings—particularly Taoism—and of those writings which deal with the encounter of the human and the divine. With an approach derived basically from Judaism, Buber became, in the traditional sense, a commentator of the Bible, and, in these early years, he published books on Oriental wisdom as well as translations of Ḥasidic texts.

Buber's is not a pure translation of Ḥasidic writing but a creative transliteration; it is, therefore, his own poetic-philosophical product. His first Ḥasidic books were written in Florence, and appeared in 1905-6. Very important, at this phase of his Ḥasidic studies, was the experience of seeing the actress Eleonora Duse on the Italian stage, an experience providing the first insights into the duality principle, the "I and Thou"—as symbolized in the stage and reality, the national and the individual, the dramatic hero and his interpreter on the stage, and the secret realm of word and answer. This source helped Buber in his first attempts to differentiate between man and God and man and creature and to make him aware of the mystery of language as a means of expressing the inexpressible.

This same polarity which Buber saw in the tension between life and stage, he thought also to exist in Ḥasidism. He encountered this polarity in the great Ḥasidic exponent, Baal-Shem, the God-seeker whom God addresses and who responds to God, as though one needed the other as complement. In this contrasted balance Buber saw the symbol for Israel itself: the calling of the infinite and the answer of the finite; the exchange of question and answer, address and response. Thus, the knowledge of Ḥasidism became to Buber the knowledge of Judaism and the life of man before God.

Ḥasidism was significantly relevant to the newly developing religious attitudes in nineteenth-century Europe, where—without any awareness of Ḥasidism—other attempts had been made to purify religious thinking from dogma and to rediscover original Christianity. Leonhard Ragaz, for example, one of the representatives of modern Christian theology, spoke of a "realization of God in the world."[2] Likewise, one might call Ḥasidism the realization of an active mysticism. Its essence, however, is not the mystic ecstasy found in unity with God, but action. Man enters into his surroundings with an act and considers even the absence of an act as his response. The specific makeup of the individual determines the essence of his deed. Every thing and every hour can become permeated with meaning and thus holy. Man is responsible not only for his own fate but also for that of God in the world. Man's task is to be aware of the meaning of the completeness of life and to mend the world where it seems broken. Ḥasidism proclaims the ethos of the concrete present, directed toward the Kingdom of God. Man contributes with his daily work toward this Messianism, and his striving is more significant than the actual arrival of that Messianic time. In these efforts toward building a better world, one of the powerful elements of existence is the word, and great strength is contained in the words of the legend and the myth. Buber saw these spiritual forces at work not only in the legends of Ḥasidism but, through his intensive studies, also in the folk tales, legends, and epics of Finland and China.

From 1905 to 1912, Buber edited the journal *Gesellschaft* (Society). In this publication can be found suggestions for a practical application of Buber's ideas which he developed in his studies for the improvement of society. Since life, to Buber, was always action, he thought that the individual's role within society, correctly applied, should serve its culture. Simultaneously with his Hasidic studies, his interest in non-Jewish religious trends, and his suggestions for social changes, Buber kept alive his love for the living literature of his day and joined the *Thursday Society* to which belonged authors like Oskar Loerke, Micah Berdyczevski, Franz Orlik, Gerhart Hauptmann, Emil Strauß, and Franz Mombert, who exerted a certain influence on Max Brod and Franz Kafka.

As a foundation for the cultural direction of his Zionism, Buber stressed the importance of learning Hebrew. Herzl's Zionism stresses the relation to one's surroundings; Buber's is reality of Judaism in the individual, who is a link to past and future, and an obligation that develops from this "belongingness." Of primary importance to Buber's Zionism is the individual's contact with his fellow men and his own illumination because of this mutual relationship. To Buber, this mutuality was the basis of Zionism in particular and of a sensible nationalism in general, and it might even show other nations the way. What Buber wanted was an "ethical rejuvenation" of nationalism, a mixture of world contact and spiritual values directed toward the future.

In Buber's analysis of the qualities of the Jew and Judaism, man, as the servant of God, contributes to the salvation of the world, even in modern Jewry, because of the polarity in the Jewish soul which, in opposition to its surroundings, strives for oneness. In post-biblical days, these characteristic features found expression in the communities of Essaeans, in original Christianity, in the Cabbala, and in Hasidism. Hasidism, one of the last Judaic manifestations, means practicing of Judaism in exile within a most hostile environment. Strains of this form and traditional interpretations of Judaism exist even in most recent times in individuals and group settlements, but the discrepancy with the outside world—and the attempt to assimilate to it—is nowadays even more pronounced, causing a struggle within the individual between his own legacy and the cultures of the adopted lands, between the consciousness of Diaspora existence and the attempt to overcome it. As certain episodes in history show, the penetration of individuals or groups into those other cultures frequently ended in catastrophe for the entire Jewry.

The other direction for the Jewish community, as opposed to attempted assimilation, is the rejuvenation that should occur in its own land, Palestine. But Buber believed that only with a spirit of Judaism that is permeated by the variety of elements acquired in the centuries of exile—elements which contribute to the vitality of contemporary Jews—is there any hope for settlement in the biblical land and for a fulfillment of the special function of the Jews among the peoples of the earth. He believed that any attempt at political contest with world powers would forfeit the special mission of creating unity in peaceful coexistence and be doomed to failure. In view of the most recent conflicts between Jews and Arabs, which, at the time of this writing, still continue, it is probably prophetic that the only solution Buber envisioned for the Middle East was a Jewish-Arab collaboration. He wrote of this unity as of the true meaning of Zionism in his journal *Der Jude*, published in 1916. But he found no echo, mainly because World War I was raging at that time.

Buber was convinced that great sacrifices would be required to end the Diaspora which, despite its cultural achievements, would eventually—because of its unnatural growth—lead to inner decay. The task of the Jews in Palestine—as Buber outlines it in *Der heilige Weg* (The Holy Path), 1917—would be to build a Jewish community whose members live in their own land. But most Zionists did not want to hear of such a role assigned to Judaism. They wanted the proper conditions to develop without being different from other nations. Once more at the end of World War I, Buber cautioned against the craving for superiority among nations. According to him, it was not important that the individual nation accomplish a goal for the sake of the nation's own profits. He felt that the Jews' striving should be replete with spirit and that only then would they be able to survive; for, as he says: on the day we will be like other nations, it will be the "defeat of Zionism."[3] Buber wanted, then, the remaking of the whole person as a logical continuation of the Jewish tradition, and he desired the proper position of the individual in a "Hebraic Renaissance," in order to build a community of work and mutual aid.

From 1919 to 1921 Buber belonged to *Hapoël Hazaïr*, a Zionist group espousing the cause of a revolutionary colonization. During these and subsequent years, some of its best members went to Palestine to settle and to till the soil. These first Ḥaluzim (Jewish pioneers) showed much enthusiasm and wanted the creation of a free human community. Youth no longer dreamed of books and theories, but of action and realization. Buber's definition of this realization is indicated in *Der heilige Weg*, where he speaks of "a rebirth of total man, of the

community as the realization of the divine in the coexistence of men."[4]
Young people going to Palestine became farmers, abandoning their
bourgeois professions, taking the step from industry to agriculture,
from abstract learning to communion with the earth and the rhythm of
nature. The new *kvutzot* (first Socialist settlements) arose, under the
influence of the youth movement and the leadership of men like Gustav
Landauer.

Buber suggested that religious inclination, developing within its own
culture, should be the goal of the new generation of the "tilling Jews,"
who were seeking to confront God and to build upon their own
heritage in Palestine. In the shadow of Achad-Haam, Buber admonished
Zionists not to follow the "dis-spirit of Europe" but the ideal of
heroism in work. He asked for a return to the land of the Jews because
of the historical and spiritual ties, not in order to oppress or displace
the other nations there, but to live with them in economic-cultural
community.

In 1921, when Buber and his friends attempted to found a "Jewish
Society for International Understanding," they proclaimed "brother-
hood of all free peoples beyond all national and nationalistic goals." A
new communion of all nations was to bring about the inner change of
every nation by living according to the true community within each;
exploitation must be replaced by education. This should be the idea
and the goal in the personal and public life of the new Jewish
community. In 1925, *B'rith Shalom* (lit., Covenant of Peace) was
founded to further the peaceful coexistence of Arabs and Jews. In this
envisioned group existence, people would live in mutual acceptance and
comprehension, forming a unity of souls and thus living in union with
God. Buber advocated the fusion of freedom and tradition for the Jews
and—on a more general plane—the unification of nations to avoid world
wars. He never abandoned his ideals and throughout his life he was
guided by this "religious Socialism."

The mid-1920's found Buber withdrawn from all political activities.
More and more steeped in the Bible and its interpretation, he began,
together with his friend, Franz Rosenzweig, the enormous undertaking
of translating the Bible into German. In a completely new approach,
they tried to adapt the meaning, rhythm, and tone of the Hebrew
language to German. When Rosenzweig died after a lingering illness in
1929, Buber, by himself, continued this incredible task for most of his
life. The occupation with the Bible led him to lecturing, teaching, and
writing commentaries. As a literary result, one of his most important

books of Bible interpretation, *Königtum Gottes* (The Kingdom of God), was published in 1932.

With the events in Germany in 1933 and with Buber's dismissal by the Nazi regime from the University of Frankfurt, he withdrew to the little German town of Heppenheim an der Bergstraße, where for five years he was a constant source of assistance for many who sought his consolation and advice. In 1938, he left for Palestine and until his very last years taught social philosophy at the Hebrew University in Jerusalem.

When Buber died in the summer of 1965, at the age of eighty-seven, he left behind not only writings on an amazing variety of subjects but also the memory of his spoken wisdom, and—as his greatest legacy—the influence of his lived life, of which one can truly say with his own words: "The spirit and life are united in the deed of man." The question is whether Buber's vision of the future which is to be "built on the dignity of man and is prepared by his deed" will come to pass. Surely, mankind would profit by living according to Buber's teachings: to lead a life of the spirit, yet one which is concrete, binding, and to be started anew when the path becomes worn. There should be no division between everyday and the festive day, between idea and life; there should only be responsibility for man, in whose life every moment can be full of decision.

CHAPTER 2

The Personality

IT is difficult to classify Buber with regard to any traditional discipline. When Buber was asked whether he was a philosopher, theologian, or any other specialist, he answered that he regarded himself "atypical." Not only personal contacts with people and formal studies but also political events helped shape his unique philosophy. World War I was incomprehensible to him, even irrelevant at first. But by trying to cope with the shock of the war, Buber, in time, expressed and clarified his position within a philosophical context. However, he felt that he could not categorize this event until this experience had become part of the past and thereby classifiable as history, as an object, and as part of the past—as an *It*. By having distanced such an immediate experience, he could reaffirm a belief which could not have existed in proximity to disaster.

In trying to cope with a historical catastrophe that had befallen man in a world of God, Buber first sought to redefine "belief"; and, as he did so, he became aware of his departure from traditional interpretations. "Belief" is customarily thought to be the domain of theology, and theology is the teaching about God. Buber, however, did not feel authorized to teach about God, and he felt that he could deal with God only in reciprocal contact with man. When trying to explain man, Buber had to consider him in confrontation with God, and there he met with a difficult problem. On one hand, God cannot be part of any logical explanation; on the other hand, God's acts cannot be separated from events in history. Historical acts, to Buber, are permeated with God's will and, in consideration of this duality, reflect his contemplation and deductions.

The foundation of Buber's thinking is an anthropological philosophy, in which any theological element is not to be taken in the traditional sense but as the belief in a man-God-experience. Such "philosophy," perceived through experience, communicates a condition in which the name of God is not replaced by a concept. Buber speaks of an encounter as the basis of communication. His theme as experiencing thinker is never suitable to become an extensive system; his supposition for all philosophizing is the duality of the *I-Thou* and *I-It* as primal words (see Chapter 3), and Buber's only interest was to become himself fully aware of this duality and to make it known to others. He did not want to deal with Being metaphysically, like a pure philosopher, but with man's double relationship to Being. His question as to how man is possible is answered by the reality of this relationship, and man should never desire to go beyond his own experience. Man must constantly reconsider his position: "I say to the one who hears me: 'It is your experience. Remember it, and what you cannot remember, dare to attain it as experience.' "[1]

Buber has no doctrine to offer but is engaged in "conversation." His basic conclusions are derived from his concept of the "primal distance of man" as a precondition of all human relationships. Man perceives the objects of his surroundings not only as part of himself but also as having their own existence. This first observation of which man is capable—and which differentiates him from other creatures—is not a reflective conduct, but man's primal act, which is also essential for establishing a relationship. Man can dismiss that which surrounds him by its removal to the position of an *It*. If he has chosen for himself that which "really" exists as he himself does, he communicates with this reality as being his *Thou*. Unlike the animal, bound in its own physicalness, man sees his surroundings as an other-ness, as Being in itself and out of itself; he becomes a spectator not only because the other-ness is meaningful to him and affects him but also because it *is* "over there." It is this ability of perceiving that distinguishes man from animal.

The question is how to transmit this recognition of man's special role to others. How can Buber use his principle pedagogically? In this respect, he is often criticized because he neither followed a tradition nor developed his own system of ethics. He says: "If I would try to categorize my views, I would hurt their essence."[2] Buber objects to the critics who want the teachers to give directives about how to walk on a road. To him, not the manner of walking, but the direction should be indicated by the teacher. As for the manner, everyone has to discover and acquire it by himself. Moreover, this direction is entirely self-contained and not dependent on prescribed principles or a system of ethics. Everyone has to accept for himself those ethical postulates that are meant for him, and only for him, to walk his path. Therefore, no ethical norm has absolute claim on a person, and, ultimately, everyone is responsible only to his own conscience.

One might criticize Buber for making the individual the only—rather uncertain—judge of his obligations because he replaces the "absolute" values with individual decisions. But, to Buber, every situation is a new one; therefore, no code can justify a given solution. Because each man's conditions and evaluations are distinctly his own, he must himself arrive at his decisions.

Buber denies that his ethics are meant for a "higher man"; indeed, special norms for a spiritual elite do not have any meaning to him, for what God pronounces as His will must be heard by each individual, its urgency being apparent in the fact that man feels himself addressed and compelled to respond. Although Buber does not castigate those who live in the tradition of their ascendants, he does reject those who "hold on to a tradition of a God-commandment, without really and truly being concerned about God."[3]

From early youth, Buber had respect for the religious feeling of every person, including the simple man who faces God without intellectually understanding his own inclinations. For Buber, only the sincerity of intent mattered, and the direction, and truthfulness to one's self was even more important than the objective. With everyone having a chance to improve, nobody was to be considered unredeemable, provided there was mutual exchange in dialogue. In this light, Buber did not regard Hitler as his antagonist, because he considered anyone like Hitler to be incapable of either addressing man or listening to him. To be sure, Hitler could cause destruction with his words; but, despite this power, his words hovering over the world produced no response and could, therefore, not be heard. Buber considered Hitler the incarnation of a destructive power; no dialogue was possible with such a negative force because there exists no equivalent of such diabolic capacity in human communication.

Even more unexpected was Buber's opposition to the execution of Adolph Eichmann after the Jerusalem trials. Like Hitler, Eichmann was not classifiable within the range of human behavior; therefore, since there could be no exchange in word or deed, Buber felt that there was no sense in adding to a man's unspeakable excess another crime by executing him. As far back as 1928, Buber had argued against the death penalty, which he considered a kind of murder which does not even have passion as a basis. A crime committed in cold blood must have self-destructive effects on the executioners because this type of murder represents chaos and moral disruption.

Concerning the planned extermination of Jews in Germany, Buber said, when he was presented with the peace prize of the German book trade (1953): "With [the Nazis] I have the dimension of human existence only as a semblance in common; they have detached themselves from the human realm so immensely into the sphere of monstrous inhumanity inaccessible to my power of imagination that not even hatred could rise in me. And what am I to take it upon myself to 'forgive!' "[4]

Buber, having lived within the range of German culture for so many years, could not simply turn away from the Germans who were held responsible for the holocaust of World War II and the extermination of millions of people. Even though he could not help thinking first of those who did not rebel against the existence of concentration camps, he was far from castigating all Germans, and he preferred to single out those who refused to execute the Nazi commands and went to their death. For those Germans he had nothing but respect and love.

The fact that there were many Germans opposed to the crimes committed during the Hitler regime even gave Buber a certain hope for future generations and the survival of mankind, although, in his opinion, until now man is far from having reached this ideal state. Since in view of the cold war waged by today's dominant powers, man's concept of his dangerous reality has been strengthened, Buber pleaded to direct this awareness toward a "great" peace which must differ from nonwar. According to him, a true peace has never really existed in modern times. What has been considered peace has always been a pause laden with fear and hope, but only a pause between two wars. Since World War II, man does not even think of peace but of a cold war declared in permanence. Having reached today's seemingly insurmountable crisis gives cause for hope; for, to Buber, there is only one alternative: the destruction of civilization or its rebirth. And he firmly believed that it was not war that has brought about the crisis; but, vice versa, that the crisis of modern man has brought forth this horror of war that was followed by a nonexistent peace.

As a counterpart to war, Buber suggested the word exchange, a dialogue in which, in order to solve political controversies, men do not only speak to each other but truly yearn to understand each other. War, to him, begins where, and because, language ends. In war, an illusory decision is sought by killing each other, in what might be called a "judgment of God." War has replaced speech with a battle cry because men have not tried to listen to speech. If they had listened, war would have become a questionable solution to them; for the words of both factions would have convinced each side that human conflict cannot be solved by means of murder.

Buber argues that nowadays the relationship of man to the word is shaken, and he sees today's dilemma immediately tied to language. A person can really speak to another only when the speaker knows that the other truly receives his word. Buber saw this failure of communication also in another realm, namely in that of prayer: man has difficulty praying, not in the sense of expressing belief that there is a God, but in simply addressing Him. This lack of man's confidence in himself, in mankind, and in God is the source of our "inner sickness of the sense of existence." And Buber believed that because of this loss of confidence, a pseudo-peace could enter into men's lives. The postwar trauma which, according to all expectations, should stress the senselessness of war and the necessity of eliminating differences of opinion, has been drowned out with noisy speeches in our present nonwar situation. There have been debates of representatives of states which have nothing to do with word exchange. They address a "faceless public" in conferences and meetings, where the directness of question and answer is abolished. Buber believed only in a genuine dialogue to cure the ills of our time, despite all the differences between men. Contrasts cannot be abolished, but a man can honor and respect the differences which he finds in others. On such a basis there can be communication between people, and it must be instigated by those who, in every nation today, fight the "counterhuman." Those who oppose such a dialogue are, to Buber, the opportunists who enjoy the separation of nations; they are the real counterhumans or subhumans, who are the enemies of all who believe in a humanity of the future.

Buber believes that men, in order not to be destroyed, must become master of the situation. In seeking a salvation or facing destruction, a man who is falling or mankind that is failing must call upon their primordial strengths and accomplish *t'shuvah* (a very vital term in Buber's language and in Judaism). It means: return, turning, renewal, cleansing of the soul having reached the bottom, where new direction is given to a force which is positive but needs impetus, guidance, and goal. As the problem concerns a person, it must also concern the species of man in his choice between decadence or complete renewal.

Satan in Hebrew means "hinderer"; and, Buber, who finds this word a good one to apply to the adverse in man and in humanity, warns that the satanic element must not hamper man in achieving his goal for the future. Buber wants uninhibited dialogue as a basis for mutual trust; for respect and confidence of one nation for another do not begin with a defense system of monstrous weapons. And Buber, a man thought to live in a special world, warns in very realistic terms of the danger of our atomic age. He suggested that man should attempt the difficult task of speaking to politicians and making them listen, in order to avoid the destruction of mankind. Politicians must stop playing games, where lives are at stake, and where eventually both partners lose. If they will not stop now, Buber warns the people of the world, the course of events will no longer depend upon man's will. The "war-playing" will have received enough impetus to destroy entire countries and peoples, "until there will be nothing to be destroyed and no one who can destroy." The basic law of all gambling, be it in war or in politics, is that "the chance of winning must not be smaller than the risk involved." In our time, the "risk" is enormous and the chance "zero," unless immediate steps are taken; for Buber firmly believed that there was still time to save modern civilization.

Because Buber realized that there have always been conflicts and that there are limitations as to how to deal with them, he suggested a compromise which, at the moment, seems to offer the only reasonable solution. This "compromise," which Buber also advocated for a peaceful Arab-Jewish coexistence, first in Palestine, and then in Israel, is not a synthesis. Buber does not mean dualism, where the elements are hostile to each other; he means polarity and duality, that is to say, an existence, side by side, of diversified forces. This duality principle is to be considered Buber's motto of existence in his written and spoken words.

CHAPTER 3

The Dialogical Principle

I   *Discussion of the Dialogical Principle*
as Affirmed and Realized Before Buber

THE essence of Buber's philosophy is the dialogical principle, his unique I-Thou and I-It relationship. Other men before him believed in this polar existence of man, and in his *Geschichte des dialogischen Prinzips* (History of the Dialogical Principle) Buber traced the developments of these thoughts and their influence on him. In discussing his philosophical predecessors, Buber emphasizes the elements he has in common with them; but, being extremely critical of certain aspects of their theories, his own view is clarified and in this crystallization becomes totally his own. His new principle is, therefore, not a mere synthesis of previous thought.

The philosophers, educators, and poets who dealt with the dialogical aspect of human relationship agree that every human being needs the contact with the other, his Thou, and that he can grow only in this relationship. The I-Thou relationship, to them, is the origin of all human development. In the eighteenth century, Friedrich Heinrich Jacobi, the German writer concerned with a "philosophy of feeling," wrote: "Without the Thou, the I is impossible."[1] Fifty years later, the German philosopher and pupil of Friedrich Hegel, Ludwig Feuerbach, said: "The conscience of the world is communicated to the I through the conscience of the Thou," and "the true I is the I that confronts a Thou and becomes to the other his Thou."[2]

Feuerbach replaces Jacobi's rather mystical I-Thou concept, whose entity is considered as God, with an anthropological substitute: "The entity of I [man's reality] and Thou [man's image of God] is man." Søren Kierkegaard, emulating Feuerbach's concept of reality, believes in God's dealing with man as an individual; but the relationship is unevenly distributed, since man depends upon God. In Kierkegaard's existential thinking, the human Thou never becomes absorbed, not even partially, in the divine; for, to him, there can be no even or uneven exchange of relationships, neither from above nor from below. There is an abyss of Being between Thou and Thou, and man's discovery of I and Thou is not an interrelationship, but an I that is dependent upon a Thou in theistic devoutness. Such dependency of the I upon a Thou appears to be monologue rather than dialogue to the neo-Kantian German-Jewish philosopher Hermann Cohen, who continues Jacobi's exclusive way of thinking, but intends a more existential interchange of I and Thou when he says: "The discovery of Thou brings about consciousness of my I";[3] for he believes that the personality of the I is brought to the fore through the Thou. And, in this sense, he believes, a correlation of man and God can function only when a correlation exists between man and man.

Franz Rosenzweig, a pupil of Cohen, shows his teacher's influence in his *Stern der Erlösung* (Star of Redemption). To Rosenzweig, the Thou is essentially spoken; and, using God's question to Adam—"Where art Thou?"—Rosenzweig asks: "Where is such a Thou, independent and free before the hidden God, in whom he can discover himself as I?" From this, Rosenzweig concludes: "I have called Thy name. Thou art mine." Here God is the instigator of the whole dialogue between Him and man's soul.

The Catholic philosopher Ferdinand Ebner speaks of the "I-solitude" as an existential, and not an original or primal, state; it is the "result of the estrangement from the Thou." The mystery of language establishes, in his view, a constantly new approach in the relationship of I and Thou. More radical than Kierkegaard, Ebner is not able to find the Thou in man; and according to him, the only thought that keeps man from perishing altogether is the idea that "there is only one Thou, and that is God." Even though Ebner also speaks of the love of man to man, for him all vanishes before the love of God. Like Kierkegaard, Ebner is a-cosmic in his love of man, and in the end, man, to him, remains, anthropologically speaking, alone.

Buber, on the other hand, being influenced by Ḥasidic thinking, speaks of the dialogue from above to below and from earth to heaven. These dialogic thoughts are first expressed in his introduction to *Die Legende des Baal-Schem-Tov* (1905), where he delineates the difference between myth and legend. In pure myth, there is no differentiation of beings. The hero stands on a step different from God; he is not confronting God. He and God are not the I and the Thou. The God of the myth creates; He sends out the created one, the hero. The God of the legend, however, summons the prophet, the saint. A legend is a myth of call and response, the myth of I and Thou, of the summoner and the summoned, of the finite being who enters the infinite, and the infinite who needs the finite: man and God complement each other. A legend is the dialogical principle exemplified; both, man and God, touch each other silently. But the difference between the partners continues, and the independence of man is preserved.

These thoughts are later continued in the preface to *Der große Maggid und seine Nachfolge* (The Great Maggid and His Succession), where Buber expressed the view that Jewish teachings are based totally on the double-directional relationship man-I and God-Thou, that is, on mutuality, on encounter. Buber's first attempts to differentiate the poles of a dialogical principle appeared in *Daniel* (1913). In this work, Buber distinguishes between orientation which clarifies and realization which represents the world of *It*, and one can already recognize in *orientation* the I-Thou, in *realization* the I-It of later works, though still not clearly divided. Buber brought these ideas to culmination in his philosophic-poetic volume, *Ich und Du* (I and Thou), on which he began to work as early as 1916.

Buber considers I-Thou as an indivisible bond between man and man, and between man and God. Desire and need for human and divine dialogue takes place in the concreteness of man's existence. Buber's views differ greatly from those of Karl Jaspers, whom he criticizes severely, especially with regard to the chapter on "existential enlightenment" in Jaspers' *Metaphysics*. Buber considers Jaspers' ideas a peculiar combination of transcendence and concreteness which do not recognize the endless possibilities of the Thou that cannot, and should not, limit any man in his dialogical search. To Jaspers, Thou becomes existential through a philosophizing person; if there is no partner, Thou proceeds untouched, without communication. Buber, on the other hand, believes that the Thou that is between man and man is the same as the Thou that comes to us from the divine and goes to the divine from us. Of greatest importance in this mutuality—not intrinsic in each partner—is the biblical marriage of divine and human love in a double commandment. This interrelationship combines the transparence of the finite Thou with the mercy of the infinite which reveals itself wherever, whenever, and however it desires.

As for Buber, Thou applies to both man and divinity. When man is not summoned by the divine power, he can only approach God through his own efforts in prayer. The philosopher may feel privileged in his philosophical existence to consider God a hidden entity that cannot be approached by man, but—this is where Buber criticizes Jaspers particularly—a philosopher has no right to consider a prayer dubious or foreign to man's experience.

When man does not communicate in prayer, he may be called upon from above, and in Buber's *Zwiesprache* (Dialogue), the importance of this singular address is pointed out. The modern philosophy of Jaspers believes that the world is a rather undecipherable existence, that transcendence represents a foreign power speaking to existence in symbols, and that a consciousness of transcendence excludes the possibility of thinking of God as Person. To make divinity a Thou means, to Jaspers, to touch transcendence. God, therefore, may be everything except a person, because to be a person means to be aware of himself, of being such a person within himself. If the divinity needed man for communication, Jaspers feels, such a divine Thou would prevent communication among men; and transcendence, brought too close to the human realm, would lose its value. In other words, a person praying, wanting to address the superior Being would degrade the latter and inhibit in himself the ability to communicate with his fellow man.

These ideas are completely adverse to the thinking of Buber, to whom man's freedom of communication is innate and represents the basis or bases for his purpose and goal of existence. Man speaks to man *because* he can speak to God, and vice versa; and Buber believed that the love of God can begin only with the love of man.

II   *Formulation of the Dialogical Principle in Buber's Early Works*

Directional Strength. The first traces of Buber's dialogic principle appear in the symbolic-poetic book, *Daniel*, written in 1913. In this work, composed of dialogues, Buber develops his thoughts on the mutuality of address and answer, of an *I* and a *Thou*, and he defines man's role in the recognition of a fluidum emanating from the essence of Being. Buber had, therefore, to be concerned with considerations of many philosophers before him; and, like them, he posed the question about the nature of reality; where man stands in nature, and about the source of man's creativity.

In trying to answer these questions, Buber does not seek to develop a set of theories; he is interested only in the intimate relationship between man and the phenomena of his surroundings and in man's inexpressible and inexhaustible curiosity about the ingredients of his existence. He investigates man's contact with the essence of Being and the possibility of a mutual exchange which he tries to clarify with examples in nature, where an interchange may exist between this essence of Being and man's inner view. Buber writes: *"Here*, where I held the stick, and *there*, where the staff met the bark—, I found just the same *I* where I met the tree."[4]

The tree-contact is the symbol for dialogue: the *I* holds the stick forming the word that is intended for the unmistakable other. *He*, the other, accepts this pure, intangible vibration, and the vibration participates in receiving the word of the *I*. Thus, in turning to the other, the *I* embraces him who, in relationship, becomes *Thou*. The fluidum existing between *I* and *Thou* represents an inexpressible exchange with the unknown. This exchange is the basis of relationship, but man must come to his particular conclusion and find the direction peculiar to him. Buber expresses these ideas in *Daniel*'s "Dialogue on the Mountain" between Daniel and the woman, where sleep, taken as symbol of the "unknown," is discussed as a pleasurable state of sinking into unconsciousness and of subsequent awakening. Because man cannot rise into the spaceless, he creates for himself his own confrontation with the night, the unknown. Within the glance of his life span, man tears from the infinity of night's directions his own night; and he uses it as a bridge from the essence of his own existence to the essence of night, which represents the essence of Being.

Unlike the eternal, man needs direction, and his path toward the eternal is such direction. Buber's ideas are similar to the Hasidic road towards the Messianic age, but they are concerned with every man, not merely with the specific group of Hasidim; he sees the chance of touching the eternal for every human being. On Buber's path, man does not proceed above earthly things, but anywhere he can have the experience of any thing that might open the gate of his *Thou*. The magic which opens this gate is the perfection of direction. Direction must be filled with strength. Either one of these elements—direction or strength—would be incomplete: strength by itself would only add profusion; direction only, applied by itself, would merely add meaning to experience. However, in combining these two elements in directional strength, Buber says, man penetrates into substance, into entity itself. "With all your directional strength receive the tree, give yourself up to it. Until you feel its bark like your skin, and the falling of a twig from the trunk like the yearning in your muscles ... until you recognize your children in the soft blue cones. Then, indeed, you will be transformed."[5] In this transformation, man's direction does not cease, and he experiences through it the tree and attains unity in the tree: "And around your direction is formed a being, a tree, so that you experience its entity. ... It is planted from the earth of space into the earth of the soul."[6] Thus, man may touch eternal life in a tree.

Buber uses Orpheus as symbol of directional strength which helps fulfill man's existence and, at the same time, makes him reach into the realm of Being. In this connection Buber also introduces the idea, very vital to him in his later works, about the renewal of man that has come out of conflict. According to Buber, Orpheus descends into Hades, not to be reunited with his beloved, but to die with Dionysus, who is Hades. Orpheus goes into ecstatic death in order to be resurrected with the dynamic force of Dionysus, and thus to fulfill the act of renewing. Music, incarnated in Orpheus, is the purest utterance of the directed soul. The Orphic soul immortalizes the magic song which is the result of direction.

The ordinary soul entering worldly existence is exposed to a multitude of happenings which surround it everywhere and could destroy it. Only because of its strength can the soul resist this "whirl," but such resistance is not the traditional self-preservation that adapts to an orderly system of causality and purpose. Buber believes that the searching soul does not stay within a given order, but deep down, stripped of all attributes of adhesiveness, the soul is ready to encounter the whirl because it is equipped with its very own "magic of direction." Direction is a primeval force which moves the human, always choosing one among the infinity of possibilities that can be realized by this particular soul. As Buber says "The soul takes off the net of directions, of space and time, of cause and purpose, of subject and object, and accepts only its magic. Powerful is the soul that encounters the whirl, banishes it magically without being destroyed."[7] Reality thus is not arranged but revealed, and a soul that is directed is a function and a necessity of nature.

Orientation and Realization. If directional strength is the prerequisite for man's attempt to fulfill his existence and achieve a higher goal, orientation and realization are man's polar means of expressing the experiences that come to him. Orientation, to Buber, shows man's readiness to be exposed to the experience. Realization means the workability of the event itself that stimulates man's creativity. To have a place in man's accomplishment, both orientation and realization have to be coupled. Realization is a first hint, in Buber's world, of *It*; to make the object, or the *It*, a part of man's encounter, he needs the orientation. Only then, in this *I*-relatedness, the *It* may become his Thou.

In the "Dialogue above the city" of his *Daniel*, Buber speaks of the double function of orientation and realization and relates them to man's experience. Man makes his experience a thing in space, "with the air column above and the magnetism of the Earth below."[8] Experience is an event in time, and man pushes it between an *after* and a *before*, where the event is squeezed by past and future. Previously, the experience was an object, as is "God to man and man to God." Man breaks this experience in the middle, in order to save its seed, and calls the pieces the perceiver and the perceived. When fitted, the resultant knowledge is pronounced to be truth; but it is not reality. Man takes out of the experience that which his orientating and realizing function has unfolded. When still unformed, he experiences but does not possess. In order to lead to knowledge and the memory of having taken possession, experience is man's bridge to form-giving. Having passed that bridge, experience becomes reality and cognition; but the event itself is like lightning. Man cannot call it and look at it, and even less can the structure of cognition be called a reality. Reality, in its general interpretation, is the sum total of the perceived and the perceivable, which is considered the existing.

Realization means to refer the event only to itself, whereby the spiritual strength of man becomes creative. Effective reality comes from the man who, entirely orientated, is ready for realization. In realizing, he is creative. He who would only realize would fuse in God; he who would only orientate, in referring only back to his *I*, would dissolve into nothingness. Orientation and realization belong together "like procreation and pregnancy."

In communal life, achieved reality must be placed in context with cognition, and individual realization must be followed by attempts of adjustment. Whoever has the most active strength of realization is most creative. His realization is a series of climactic points touching the eternal. But also in his orientation lives the spark of reality. Unbroken strength of realization is most prominent in primitive man and the child because—in their lack of experience—their capabilities of orientation have not yet matured. Primitive man and the child, in their proximity to nature, are *still* masters of reality; the genius, incapable of moments of inactivity, is *already* master of reality.

The realization of cognition creates the essential form of existence. "The thing and I, both are contained in that which thus has been created." Here both find their reality, and all cognition is an inkling of unitedness. Orientation by itself distorts; realization completes. Nothing separate is, by itself, real; everything separate is only a precondition, and creative hours are uniting hours. Buber considers the hero, the poet, and the prophet united within themselves. The mystery of each of these is his ability of communion. He is real because, in his exceptional moments, he is part of what is real, and his reality is for all and none. This reality *is*, whether or not it is seen. This power of creativity—though reduced—exists in every man, not only in the chosen.

Properly exercised, orientation and realization in the deeds of man would improve the human race. But Buber thinks that man, in the present world, wants to arrive at his goals without including realization, which means that people try to give what they do not have. These "lap-children of appearance" conquer without battle. Their acts are similar to those of realization, and they are committed quickly and with elegance. They only want recognition and think of themselves as being gods because, with modern techniques, they believe that they create as God did. Man of the present world distorts reality in order to let appearance triumph; he exists, but he does not bring his life to fruition. An event that could have been one of special address is "classified" without having been grasped. People calculate which elements one event has in common with others and think they are *oriented.* On the basis of their machine-age orientation, they define what is culture, religion, progress, tradition, intellectuality. In chasing only after their own goals, they have Buber's *orientation* but lack the willingness to strive for *realization.*

This orientation without realization is the beginning of the sin against the spirit. Spirit is realization, a united-ness of the soul that is exclusive experiencing. But man today is caught in his goals, means, and in various forms of knowledge. In the security of becoming oriented, he thinks that he knows everything. The experience is grasped within itself, since it can be found on a map of earth and sky and can be defined according to names, altitude, and longitude.

Man wants security, and awareness of a goal is security. Fear overcomes many men when they are confronted with the irrational; and, instead of utilizing and realizing the *irrational* and incorporating it with the whole power of the moment into the event, they only want to safeguard their security. But all experiencing ought to be replete with danger, one that might be called a productive danger. Leading a life of realization, man would have to unbendingly begin anew, eternally dare anew. His truth would not be *possessive* but *becoming*; and he would be in process of constant change. Most men, however, in continuously assuring and adapting themselves, want to orient themselves in the world and preserve themselves in it. They construct an ark they call *Weltanschauung*; and, says Buber, they "smear up all cracks, even the windows, with tar. But outside are the waters of the living world."[9] In short, modern society lives more by preconceived slogans, which, in reality, mean separation, than by the spirit of unitedness. Buber warns that what is today semblance or appearance should be changed to a lived life which honors the happening that addresses each man; then everyone would be able to contribute with his particular orientation and realization.

The early expression of Buber's thinking, his orientation and realization, is found in *Daniel*, one of the most poetic of Buber's writings, written in a language of great simplicity yet full of symbols and allegories. As in the book of *Tao* or the words of Buddha, the stress is on the intangible aspect of man's existence and on his relationship in this world to the spirit beyond this world. The book deals with the theme of polarity, tension, and realization of man's being through his actions in many variations. What has been announced here by means of image and symbol, Buber expresses in clear, concise language, but in thoughts more philosophically oriented, in his book, *Ich und Du*, which, throughout his life, he considered the most essential work for an understanding of his ideas. It was *Ich und Du*, of all his writings, which he recommended to Dag Hammarskjöld for translation into Swedish, and it accompanied the latter on his last flight which brought tragic death.

Ich und Du goes beyond showing the evidence of man's polar existence with all its inexpressible ramifications. Buber tries in very clear, factual language to delineate his philosophy without, however, placing his ideas within philosophical categories. The book is not a culmination of philosophical schemes; it is not a scheme at all, but it amounts to a thought association that must be understood within itself, without any dependency upon theories or doctrines of previous thinkers.

Illusion and Reality. The chapter "Conversation after the Theater" in Buber's *Daniel* is not only an allegory of the unknown quality of man's existence but also a poetic interpretation of Buber's polarity concept of *Ich und Du*. He not only speaks of the mystery of illusion and reality on the stage but of the theater as a symbol of life itself. Just as a person one knows very well may, in a sudden light, be revealed to us for the first time, or just as the secret of a basic relationship to life may be suddenly recognized in the familiar face of that person, so the spectator reacts to the sudden change from the street to the darkened theater. His only connection is with the front; there is no side, no back, no *before*, no *after*. The actors appear and disappear like shadows coming from, and fading into, the edge of Being. The spectator sees a play of two-some-ness which is beyond good and evil; he observes the primeval two poles, essence and counter-essence, that are evidenced in the poles of spectator and player, which are alternately contrasted and united. In the outside world, these poles are unrecognizable; but in the theater they are naked, untarnished in gesture and voice. The chorus of figures surrounding them makes them stand out and does not diminish the fluidum between these poles of actor and spectator, and the *I* of the spirit stands in their midst to reveal their secret two-some-ness.

The spectator, like the *I* of the spirit, is in this duality, as caused and experienced by the actor, also a participant in the action on the stage. At the same time, he is aware of the other spectators as a community in which the individual represents one member of the group. Now the event on the stage confronts the *We-I* (the *I* as part of the audience-community), representing tension or contradiction with the balance on the stage which is attempted by the hero-actor. Separated by the footlights are space and the frame of the stage, time and setting, balance and action, audience and play, that is, the polarity of the imaginary and the real world. The relationship between the stage and the audience equals that of happening and perceiving. Perceiving does not take sides; it is self-contained, except for its confirmation of the happening on the stage. Perceiving becomes proclamation because the perception is willful. The audience identifies with the tragic events on stage by joining the fate of the play's personalities. One being confronts his counterbeing and, in facing his counterpole, experiences life. This interchange, to Buber, is like the grasp of the lover who not only expresses his own desire but also experiences that of the beloved one, embracing thus the most contrasting poles as his very own.

Buber considers the illusion on the stage to be complete and the fragments of Being to be a reality. Which is the more profound reality? Which power can pull man out of the polarity of his existence to place him before the strong immediacy of the polarity of the tragedy enacted on the stage? The play's impact on the actor, who represents a stage personality, colors his own self and influences his own actions. The process of the theater is unified. An actor, then, can become reality having within himself the polarity of hero and actor. His soul must be stimulated by the spark which makes, out of the experience of the individual, through his action the happening for all. He lives the fragment of action which takes on the independence of a whole, and this fragment becomes "simulacrum."

The stage personality undergoes a metamorphosis. The actor confronts the hero and does the "simulacrum," the act, which is polar. The actor changes into the hero without aping him, for he actually creates the hero anew with soul and body. The great actor does not grope; he transforms himself. He gives up his soul and regains it when penetrating into the core of the hero, and he lifts the latter's secret of personal *kinesis*—the connection peculiar to him—out of sense and action. He holds the elements which produce sounds and gestures. The substance belongs only to the one whom he plays. The actor does not experience the feeling, only its outward manifestations and the excitation in which he stands in his own self, the stimulus of his transformation containing the polarity of his self and of his hero. The source of all excitation is experience and realization, and, in his desire for unity, the actor fulfills himself in fusing the polar elements.

The player cannot divine the secret of polarity with his senses, nor can he deduce it with his thinking. He can only raise it out of the world with his transformation. With his metamorphosis he symbolically fulfills the secret movement of the world: in his acts he lives the action of the world. To Buber, the actor can be compared to the enigma of the world, which is the kinesis of the infinite, the amalgamation of sense and Being. The one who approaches the infinite from his earthly surroundings achieves the polarity by reaching out for his counterpole, just as the actor approaches the hero. Exactly as the player becomes creative in being the hero, man grows beyond himself and touches his counterpole in imitation of the unknown God. This striving for the divine is man's realization; through struggle, love, cognition, and fulfillment in two-some-ness, a unity emerges out of each pole when man reaches out for the other, contrasting one.

Ich und Du. The furthest apart, yet most intimately related poles in man are *I* and *Thou*, and in *Ich und Du* (first published in 1919; final version in 1922), Buber's most significant book in the development of the dialogic principle, he investigates the role of man as an individual within his environment, as a social being, and, finally, as an earth-bound creature trying to communicate with a superior power. The inter-relationship of man and his surroundings, of man and man, and man and God is so strong, Buber says, that there is no life which does not include these three elements: the *I* and the objective world, the *I* and the other man, and the *I* and God. Therefore, the *I* as such does not exist. There are only dual principles which exist for man, and they can be expressed in the primal entities *I-Thou*, shown in the relationship of *I* and man and *I* and God, and in *I-It* which is the *I* within the world or the *I* and the objects surrounding man.

According to Buber, the *I* is twofold, because *I* of the basic word *I-Thou* is different from *I-It*. When *Thou* is spoken, *I-Thou* is spoken also; when *It* is spoken, *I-It* is spoken also. *I-Thou* can be spoken with the entire essence, but *I-It* never, because the intimacy is not contained in one's relationship to an object. There is no *I* per se, only as it appears in *I-Thou* and in *I-It*. When man speaks *I*, he means one of the two. When he speaks *Thou* or *It*, the *I* of the one or other primal word is implied, and in speaking one of the primal words, man enters that word and lives in it.

Surroundings, activities, will, perception are the *It*. Speaking *Thou* does not have *something* as object. The *It* represents one of many objects; its only reason of existence depends on the fact that the *It* borders on other *Its*. *Thou* does not border. Speaking *Thou* establishes an immediate connection. Only experience brings to man the world of *It*, whether evident or hidden, and the man who has an experience has no contact with the world. Experience is in him, and not *between* him and the world. Man's experience is immaterial to the world, since an experience does not add anything to the world. The *I-It*, therefore, is non-mutual, one-directional, from *I* to *It* only.

The ground-word *I-Thou*, on the other hand, founds the world of relation with nature or with man, where this ground-word is speech-formed, and establishes mutuality. Man can give to the *Thou* and receive from *Thou*. Spiritual substances are being revealed, but not necessarily in speech; they are, however, speech-creating. The *I* does not necessarily hear the *Thou*, but still feels addressed by it. The *I* answers by forming, thinking, doing; the answer is given with man's essence, not with his mouth. Thus, in every sphere, man addresses the eternal *Thou*. Rare moments can establish an uncommon relationship, as when a manifestation of nature, such as a tree in *Daniel*, no longer is an *It*. This tree then confronts the *I* and becomes *Thou*, even though the *I* never finds out about the tree's consciousness.

Addressing the other as *Thou* means speaking to a *Thou* without neighbor and without distance to the *I*. Not that there is nothing except *Thou*, but everything else lives in the "light" of *Thou*. To divide such *Thou* into various attributes would mean that it is no longer *Thou*. If *Thou* Becomes He, She, or It, it is no longer a person's *Thou*. Buber says: "As long as the sky of the Thou is stretched above me, the winds of causality crouch at my heels, and the whirl of disaster congeals."[10] Buber indicates that at the moment of relatedness there is no "knowledge." As soon as there is consciousness, there is *Thou*-distance. The *Thou* is only "known" at the moment when the *I* leaves the relationship. Knowledge, therefore, is creating distance from *Thou*, and the *Thou* contains more than the *It* "knows."

The artist's creation portrays the relationship in which man, the creator, shapes his *Thou* out of the world of *It*. Accordingly, all real life is encounter. Between *I* and *Thou* there is no concept, no pre-knowledge, no fantasy. Any relationship is in immediacy, and out of the past the present can only arise when *Thou* becomes actuality. The *I* of the ground-word *I-It*, having no actuality, lives in the past. There, even a moment is without present. The *It* contains nothing but objects. Objects exist only out of their past; they are holding still, maintain a status, lacking relationship and present. Related substances are lived in the present, objectivities in the past. Buber believes that there is no isolated *I* or isolated *It*, but only the reality of man who, with his life, mingles with the world of objects and ideas.

By the same token, in man's relationship to man, *Thou* is not necessarily evidenced. If there are mutual feelings, they are possessed; only love *happens*. Feelings dwell in man, but man dwells in love. Love is between *I* and *Thou*. Love is also the responsibility of an *I* for a *Thou*, and this relationship is true mutuality. When one person negates another, he is not able to speak *Thou*. And, as far as Buber is concerned, the man who hates in immediacy is closer to relationship than the one who lacks love and hatred.

One of the human dilemmas is that a *Thou* cannot last as such and must eventually become an *It*, and what had been in the secret of mutual effect a moment ago, becomes again describable, arrangeable, the meeting point of many circles of law. A person who, an instant ago, was not experienceable, only touchable, again becomes He or She, a quantity of attributes. Then He or She is no longer, or not again, a *Thou*. Everything in the world can, either before or after its becoming a thing, appear to an *I* as his *Thou*. As Buber says, the *It* is the "pupa," the *Thou* the "butterfly."

Precursors of Mature Man. Instead of concise words which are the commonly accepted symbols of an I-Thou relationship, communication of another type may signify a more intense connectedness, as Buber sees a more direct relationship, for example, in primitive civilizations. Where Western civilization says: "far away," the Zulu expresses this thought with a symbolic allusion: "there where one screams: 'O, mother, I am lost' "; whereas the Fire Island inhabitant thinks of distance in terms of a hurt relationship, and he says: "one looks at each other, each expecting that the other offer to do what both wish but do not want to do."[11]

Because of primitive man's close relationship to nature, moon, sun, death, have great power over him. The causality of his world picture is not given within a continuity but is a constantly renewed fact, a motion without establishing direct contact. The primitive I *knows* only man and his confrontation; the world becomes his opponent and creates in him his dualistic system, because primitive man, Buber believes, cannot establish an I-Thou relationship. He does not pronounce the I-tree relation in an empirical formula as a relationship I-man and Thou-tree, but states the tree-object perception through the consciousness of man only and thus, from the start, has spoken the ground-word I-It, the word of separation.

In an even more pronounced way than primitive man, the child gives us the message of the two primal words. His spiritual reality comes from the relationship I-Thou, the primal word I-It from contrast. The prenatal child has a natural physical link with, and "longing" for, the "worldlike connectedness of the being with his Thou." As the child develops, he separates from the primeval world, to be enveloped again in this world in his dark hours when losing his personal life in sleep.

Growing into life, the child gradually exchanges his loss of connectedness to nature with a spirited relation to the world. He is learning to make this creativity of his a reality in perceiving, listening, and forming. In the encounter, a thing is revealed to him only in the power of that which is across and opposite him. The first reaction of the child is the glance at something uncertain that he molds into the recognition of something distinguishable because of his constant drive to consider everything his Thou and, if necessary, to give of his own self in order to create the proper balance in a meeting with the symbol of his encounter. According to Buber, the drive for connectedness in the child comes first, and that which confronts him complies through his unconscious efforts of creating an exchange. At the level of the child, speaking is still wordless, and only later this pre-form of Thou is objectivated because the partner has been separated. The I then arises. Buber believes that there is a drive toward relationship in the beginning of man's existence, a readiness, an inborn Thou, and that in the experienced relationships the innate Thou, at the moment of encounter, becomes reality. At his earliest stage the child accepts a Thou and later addresses Thou with the primal word I-Thou because of the inborn nature of man's drive for relationship.

As the soul in the child develops, so does his longing for Thou, with all the fluctuations in the fulfillments and deceptions of this desire, culminating in the tragedy of the child's helplessness. The infant's physicalness has come into this world without his having completely lost his ties to nature. Not until his entire substance has made contact with world-reality, and until such time that his complete fusion takes place, can a full relationship with world and man begin.

Independent Man. Having reached his independent self, man becomes the I in the Thou. The consciousness of the I crystallizes through the consciousness of the partner. The other appears in relationship to the Thou, until, detached, the I will confront itself, as it would a Thou, to take possession of itself. This I does not yet necessarily comprise the I of an I-Thou relationship, because the mere presence of the Thou does not guarantee relationship. One might almost speak of an It that is awaiting a new relationship. When the moment of such an encounter approaches, the I, now leaving its completeness of substance, becomes the experiencing subject that wills the *It* and fuses with *It.* The man who speaks I-It and places himself in front of things, experiences them as a sum total of attributes. They belong to the remembered Thou, but the things themselves only show him the structure of their attributes. From the memory of his relationship man completes the kernel which revealed itself, at one time, with all its attributes, and which is the substance. At that point, all observed things are localized as to space, time, causality, and represent the *It* of man. At the moment of mutual encounter, however, the Thou appears in such an exclusive confrontation with the I that the Thou's real dimensions and measures are uncertain. The encountering Thou effects and receives effect, not in a chain of causality but in reciprocity only, with I as Beginning and End of the happening. No measurement must or can enter, as only an It can be regulated. Anything which later develops out of Thou in the element of time becomes an It; at that point, the *It* can be coordinated. Thou does not know a coordinate system. A regulated world is not the true world order, which only at rare moments becomes apparent as a special gift to man that is immortal and yet uniquely mortal; for the content of such extraordinary historic moments cannot be preserved; but at least their strength enters creation and, from there, the cognition of man.

Buber believes that it is up to man *how* any unit of the immeasurable becomes reality. Every encounter is a sign of the world order, and each promises him connectedness with the world. The world thus is not outside but touches man's ground. When man makes this happening his object, there is no more present; but when he says Thou to the world, the world says Thou to man and renders itself to him. The world points the way to Thou, in which, says Buber, the "parallel lines of relationships meet," giving man a glimpse of eternity. Man regards the It-world as his world in space and time; the Thou-moments appear in this world as lyrical-dramatic episodes, shaking any feelings of security. But it is not enough to utter Thou. Unless the waves are simultaneously sent out from the partner, the mysterious primal word I-Thou has not been spoken. When this eternal mutual "glance" occurs, time seems to stand still (or not to exist), and man stands in the present. But no being can live in a pure present; his present has to be overcome; he can only exist in the pure past. Buber says: "Without It, man cannot live, but he who lives with It alone, is not truly man."

The history of the individual and of the species has one factor in common: the progressive increase in the It-world, that is, the material world and its spiritual, artistic, and philosophical aims being larger in every subsequent culture than in the preceding one. Man's relationships to the It-world contain experience and use; with the increase of the It-world man's capability for experience and use also grows. If the individual believes that he can use shortcuts through means and direct application instead of seeking the opportunity to establish an I-Thou relationship, the power of relatedness, which, Buber thinks, makes it possible for man to live in the spirit, decreases.

Spirit is man's communication with his Thou. Spirit is not *in* the I but *between* I and Thou, like the air we breathe. If man enters into relationship with his whole substance, he can answer his Thou. Only thus can he live in the spirit. The more powerful his answer, the more powerful his tie to the Thou. Only the silence of the spirit in which Thou is addressed can liberate Thou, as Buber says, out of the "pre-tonguely," pre-speech-formed It-world. In regarding that which confronts man, its essence is disclosed to the observer. As an It, the observed object becomes part of man's cognition. In the process of mutual observation and reciprocal penetration, this *vis-à-vis* no longer is a thing, but is exclusively present in appearance; its essence establishes bonds. This essence, freed from the It-form and regarded in an act of recognition, fulfills the fluidum between men. Out of the tension of the I-Thou and I-It confrontation arises cognition, work, image. After having become object, the It can again become present, returning to the elements whence it came, to be regarded and lived by man in the present. In this exchange Buber sees the healthy growth and improvement of mankind and world.

On the other hand, there are those who have codified, have found their answers in books, and thus have excluded themselves as encountering I. Such a person lives among the people of his society, but he has categorized his life into institutions and feelings, It-precinct and I-precinct. Institutions to him are the "outside" where one works, competes, organizes, officiates, breathes, and preaches, accompanied by other members of the human race, while feelings are the "inside" where one lives and recovers from the institutions. Such a person is delivered to his emotions which are "tasted" in their full spectrum.

Buber sometimes finds it difficult to distinguish between feelings and institutions, as for example in the institution of marriage, but the distinction can be clearly seen in public life, as, for example, in political parties, conferences, and movements. Institutions and feelings do not know the living person; institutions only know the type, feelings only the object. They do not know communal life or present, nothing but strict past, which means completion for an institution and the fleeting moment for a feeling. Neither institution nor feeling has access to real life. Institutions do not represent public life nor do feelings represent personal life. A community cannot be established by having people unite just because they have feelings for one another. To Buber, real community means to have a mutual relationship toward a living center. To be sure, feelings must exist, but no relationship is derived from them.

CHAPTER 4

The It *and the* Between *in the I-Thou World*

I *The Artist's World*

TO the artist in contemplation at the moments preceding his creations, the essence confronting him reveals its form, which is not in a God-world, but in the world of man, and wants to work through him, that is, through his inspiration. When he begins to work or, with Buber, speaks the word, this act of creation means sacrifice and risk. Sacrifice: because all must be destroyed that is not part of the immediacy of the confronting object; and risk: the I may not serve well, and the spell may, therefore, be broken.

The art image confronts the I and cannot be experienced, but only realized. Yet, the I of the artist perceives this image clearer than anything in the experienced world. The art image works in the creator as the I works in the art image. Giving the work its form is discovery. In the realization of the art product, the I discovers. The I leads an image, which receives form and substance, into the world of I, where, as a formed substance, it becomes a thing among things, in order to continue eternally, always an It, but also eternally becoming Thou when regarded and touched. The art product thus physically confronts the recipient eager to perceive an I-Thou relation. This exchange between the art product and the I is without knowledge, and the interrelationship is passivity and activity simultaneously. When the I is being addressed, the resulting action of the I is completed in a process of response. As Buber says: "I *become* in Thou, and in becoming I, I speak Thou."

The artist stands in the polarity of encounter, and at that immortal moment the tension of his own polarity, which represents his I, meets the Thou. In this unique world of Between, the work of art, which is a product of spirit and form, originates. As Buber says in *Ich und Du*: In artistic creation "form-giving is discovery."[1] In a painstaking task, in the process of forming, the artist again and again will stand in this

I-Thou relationship, until the finished product enters the world of It. A sculpture, a painting, a symphony, a poem came out of tension, and in a timeless moment, eternally repeated, is added to the world of It. Hofmannsthal says: "Painting changes space into time, music time into space."[2] Now a form, waiting for man in his single-ness or community to experience the art work, can become again his or their Thou. An unlimited continuance of this process may be an indication of how much of the original product has become part of the cultural It out of which it grew.

What was true for the creation of the art product in the past must also be true in the future, or that product will be semblance instead of creation—in terms of art, pseudo-art. But it is also necessary that the man who is the recipient of the artist's product be ready for an encounter; for the work will not come to him. He must go to that which *is*, and again at an immortal moment, it will become his Thou. Or as Hofmannsthal writes: "People demand that a poetic work address them. . . . This the higher works of art do not do, just as little as nature makes common cause with man; it [art] is there, and leads man beyond himself if he is collected and ready for it."[3]

The artist who creates in dialogue is holding his moment of encounter; for the work will not come to him. He must go to that this process Buber can speak of art as "replica," because it is not a replica of nature. It *is* nature, and its reality had to be poured into form. Thus, in the visual arts, time was conquered, but music, drama, and poetry always have to be re-created in time to become this form, which the sculptor and the painter had been able to finish in a final stroke. Drama and poetry may fulfill this form in anyone's spokenness; only music cannot be sound without a re-creation. Only through the necessary tension in the re-creating artist can the work come to the listener. This double process, however, being a phenomenon which places greater responsibility on the "middleman or -men," does not dilute the possibility and intensity of the encounter.

Perhaps because music does not have direct contact with man but needs a medium to convey its meaning to him, one might say that, without this interpretative power, music would stay within its own realm and would not enter the world of the listener. This relationship, which can only be established by a re-creator, may be the reason why Buber, who wants direct encounter, is less concerned with music than he is with the art of the word, the symbol of reality, and the atmosphere which it creates. In a number of works, particularly in

Daniel, he dealt with the phenomena of art, the artist, his tension and unity, and the receiving spectator.

Toward the end of *Daniel*, Buber gives his analysis of the meaning of an art work and the polarity which manifests itself most strongly in the poet. To Buber, all poetic work tends to drama; every lyrical work is a conversation, in which the partner speaks in a superhuman language, and what he says is the secret of the poet, who constantly makes decisions in rejecting much that might want to be created by him in favor of what he has chosen. Buber says: "Writing poetry is choosing in infinity." It is a fire that has destructive power. "Around each word there is a ring of intangible matter, depicting the sphere of infinite perishing." When Plato calls the poet the messenger of God, Buber adds that he is also the messenger of polar earth. The poet knows the poles of superstrength and the lack of it, of freedom and dependence, of union and solitude, of guilt and purity, of form and formlessness. As Buber says: "His heart is the hub in which the spokes of polarity come together; it is not dissolution, but connection, not indifference, but fertility."[4] The poet has a twofold love: love of the world with its truth of colors and tones, and love of the work, which, having grown out of the tension of generations, can dissolve and unite all tension. In his love, all contrasts become fertile. "Completion and emptiness create in the poet Heaven and Earth, word and world," and he says to the world: "This is the rainbow bridge from pole to pole." "All poetic creation is discourse, because all poetry is the forming of a polarity, a direct polarity of the soul."[5]

Buber also sees in the drama the polar situation because individuals are set against each other, and an encounter will bring about their relationship. It can provoke feelings of love, passion, jealousy, and a dilemma where a decision will lead to a solution, but more likely to an adverse act, considered a crime by human standards. The individual involved in tension with the taboos of his environment will, in the majority of cases, be tortured by feelings of guilt. The drama at its culminating point will either give a means to cope with this guilt or will convince the spectator of the inaccessibility and insurmountability of guilt in man.

The drama is presented on the stage, a delineated world of its own, and though drawn into the complications of human involvement and reenacting its tragedy, the spectator is only temporarily taken out of his own realm. There will be moments within the drama's unfolding when the person outside the stage will be aware of the discrepancy or similarity between his own life and that presented on the podium. He is entangled with his own self through the medium of someone else's self, namely that of the actor. And even though the actor may create the illusion of reality, at the moment of awakening the spectator will settle for his own life and consider the illusory world on the stage an entertainment.

Despite the illusion created through the art of writing, the novel is closer to the beholder's own life. The spectator is now in direct contact with the action. He no longer depends on a presentation of the events through the medium of a special world established on a podium. He is in more direct touch with the passion, love, or guilt of the heroes. There is no stage, no actor, no other spectator, and no dependency upon spokenness or sound. The world of the novel may be as turbulent as the real world, but it exists only in the special realm created by the artist for the reader. And since feelings are not publicly announced, as in the theater, the reader has a more direct contact and can more easily, and without any inhibitions, identify with those feelings and actions which are contradictory to commonly accepted behavior. Following the hero through all the minute details of a hunted soul, he will come to the conclusion that real guilt weighs heavier than a remembrance of the situation when it was incurred—as psychoanalysis claims—because, Buber emphasizes, real guilt lives with the person and never enters the unconscious, not because of hostile acts against social traditions but against himself.

Buber always believed in man and the importance of his imprint on the surrounding world, but he had no use for intellectual structures, methods, or clichés, be they political, social, psychological, philosophical, or religious traditions. For the same reason, words had to be separated from any preconceived meaning and be given a new impetus, be it in the spoken or in the written word, most ideally presented in a poem.

Throughout the history of man's search for an expression of the last questions about human existence, some poets were able to capture in words—and even more poignantly in what remained unsaid in their poems—the wonderment of existence and its relationship to a superior force. They, too, have had to take the words out of their daily abuse and give them a new direction. In works like Buber's *Daniel, Ich und Du*, and his poems, his groping for expression is probably as important as that of those poets who approached the word exclusively in poems. He joins them in their effort not to explain or to know, but through their artistic creation to believe in the mystery of man's polarity.

II   *Imbalance in a Relationship*

Buber speaks of some human relationships which do not contain complete reciprocity, some in nature, some among men. He thinks that the duality of man's primal words, I-Thou and I-It, is unknown to the animal, and different in the plant. The plant cannot respond but does manifest a reciprocity of Being; the entity of tree exists as being tree to the one who speaks Thou, thus representing a step toward the sphere "before the threshold" of an eventual encounter. This sphere contains both the spirit having entered the world perceived by man, the observer, and also, from the other side, the spirit that has not yet left but is ready for the world.

The animal's language, in all its richness, expresses the motion of the creature between plantlike security and spiritual daring. In the glance of the cat toward that of man, there is a short moment of transition from the It-world to the world of Thou and a sliding back into the It-world. Rilke's creatures represent the It-world, because plants and animals are observed within themselves and unrelated to each other. A contrast of Thou is established, where the I, in losing its I-ness, becomes the Thou, and in contemplation is identified with Thou. Rilke, in his effort to understand the It-world, lets the I melt into the It. Buber, however, believes in a momentary dialogue of man and creature: when the I ceases to be Thou, the momentary Thou becomes It again.

Buber says that there is a very narrow margin between this momentary dialogue and such an effort which turns out to be a monologue. The I may, for example, touch things in nature and feel their other-ness. At the moment of the awareness of the I's hands, the contact is lost. The directedness of the inclination toward mutuality has been interrupted in the awareness of the I. Instead of experiencing the other-ness of the other, he has only his own experience which does not include the other. So-called dialogue, then, becomes semblance, and interchange becomes amusement.

Buber also considers the possibility of a relationship in which the present meets the past. We know, for example, the saying of a great man who lived thousands of years ago; we know this phrase as an object whose spirit, long ago, had gone into the world and now touches us in this our life. It is even entirely possible to re-create in us the voice that spoke this wisdom, as long as the listener has the inclination of saying Thou. He will then hear the voice ringing through all the genuine words of the master. The listener will not be able to differentiate the content and rhythm of the words which previously were object, but will receive them as indivisible totality of a "spoken-ness." This post-relationship is not limited to the message of a person but can also manifest itself in man-made objects, says Buber, and he speaks of the Doric column as having meaning to us since its creation in antiquity. Its mutuality has not disappeared but only faded into the background, where it has become concrete objectivity. In the manner of this illustration, spirit, becoming word or form, grows out of an encounter of one with the other as inspiration. Nietzsche's definition of "inspiration," "Take and do not ask who is giving," is changed into "One does not ask, but one is grateful." No calculation should enter the natural flow, or else the breath of the spirit is stifled. Anyone wanting to take possession of the spirit or thinking of it as a gift specifically designed for him, would create an imbalance of exchange and destroy the encounter.

As there may exist an imbalance of relationship between man, plant, creature and the direct encounter with the world spirit, a total mutuality does not necessarily exist between men, yet can still be fruitful. A genuine Thou-relationship, for instance, can hover between teacher and pupil. A teacher has to recognize the totality of the other person without thinking of him in terms of an accumulation of qualities. He meets him always as his partner in a bipolar situation, which he must experience from the polarity of the pupil as well as from his own. This *embrace* has to awaken the I-Thou relationship in the pupil, but the *embrace* cannot originate in the same measure from the pupil, who cannot exercise the same participation in the mutual situation, except if it were in a transfer to a friendship. An educational relationship is no more mutual than is the psychotherapeutic one. The therapist may be able to assist a "diffused soul," but, according to Buber, he cannot accomplish what would be his real task, namely the regeneration of a degenerate person-center. The real change would only be possible in a partnerlike attitude from person to person. The therapist, too, simultaneously has to stand with his own pole at the other pole—that of the patient—and experience the effect of his own work. If the patient were to attempt the same *embrace*—to experience the happening at the medical pole—the relationship would end. Buber believes that, whenever an aim is to be accomplished, mutuality cannot be complete.

Buber also answers those critics who stress the unbalanced relationship of man and a superior Being by saying that all I and Thou is only appearance and a superficial principle. To them, the primeval Being into which we should sink to contemplate, is beneath I and Thou. We should be aware of the relativity of our existence and not try to fill dialogue with I and Thou, taken out of absolute Being—to them an indivisible entity—beyond our lived life. Buber denies that such Being can be reached in *experience.* In this negative kind of responsibility, Buber argues, man is only concerned with a lyrical self-assertion, and it would mean that before birth and at death only man is tied to God, but that he is disconnected and abandoned as creature at the moment of release from the Creator.

According to Buber, the entity of a person is not distinguished from entity as such. A person experiences the cessation of multiplicity as entity itself, as his fulfillment of the I-Thou happening. To Buber, entity means the two-some-ness of I and Thou, where man is in the situation of creation, which is truer than all ecstasy. This lived entity only knows dialogic living, and having become one, is not the result of an I-experience found in solitude, because life does not consist of creaturely everyday life and supreme divine moments. Entity in fulfilled living is a continuous waiting in concreteness in which, as Buber says, "one perceives the word and stammers the answer."

III   *The Between in Dialogue*

While *Daniel* and *I and Thou* concentrate on the relatedness of I and Thou and a loss of direct contact in the objective world of I-It, Buber is concerned with the phenomena of the dialogue between the partners in *Zwiesprache* (Dialogue). This book, published in its final version in 1934, is the necessary complement to *Daniel* and *I and Thou.* In the two earlier books, the focus is on the partners; in *Zwiesprache*, it is on the *Between,* the word that unites them. Buber describes the situation that exists between I and Thou, and, for him, the dialogic encounter is as a united Between, emanating from each partner. At the ideal moment, the encounter does not happen, but *is.* It is in friendship and love and may suddenly exist with a glance in a crowd in what Buber calls a "fateless swinging," even in an unspoken word.

Participating in a discussion does not necessarily mean dialogue; for, as Buber conceives it in *Zwiesprache*, there can be dialogue without sound and gesture, not only of lovers or in a mystical "together-silence," but in any confrontation with the divine spirit, be it in a religious or an artistic happening. Human dialogue can be without signal. Since man's life takes place in time-space-bound concreteness, the dialogue, at the supreme moment, may go beyond its borderlines and may be completed within a concrete experience. At such a moment, the law of understanding and opinion does not apply. It is a matter of interpreting the divine will, but no one should try such interpretation with a furtive application of intellect or sentiment. Buber does not agree with Luther and Calvin, who think that God's word must be recognized and be exclusively represented in each situation. Buber says: "The word of God comes down before my eyes like a falling star, of whose fire the meteor will speak without having to burn me, and I myself can only attest to the light, but not bring forth the stone and say: 'This is it.' "[6]

In describing the precondition for an encounter of dialogic partners, Buber distinguishes between *observing, regarding*, and *becoming aware*. The observer of man sketches as many of his traits as possible, with all his individual variants. In *regarding* him, all is arbitrariness; nothing is noted down, and no task is given to memory. One is waiting for that which will present itself and is interested only in that which is not *character* or *expression*. Observer and regarder have their disposition in common. The person observed is hereby detached from the observing person, to whom the observed is a sum of traits, and the regarder looks at a sum of events as emanation of existence. In *regarding* or *observing*, neither action nor fate are added. The observer summarizes, while the regarder looks behind and beyond appearance. The categories of *regarding* and *observing* are no longer applicable at the supreme hour of encounter; for the totality of man is inexpressible while he is speaking to the partner. The result of what has been spoken exceeds *observing*. The *I* cannot describe the whole person who speaks; or else, it would be the end of listening. The only responsibility of the listener lies in his answering, whether at once or whenever or how it may take place. This response Buber calls the *awareness*, which can come from man or anything alive or dormant in nature, since "nothing can refuse to become vessel to the word." The limit of the possibilities of the dialogic principle is the same as that of *awareness*.

Man exists as if encased in armor. The world speaks always to us. But only at certain moments the armor is pierced. Every day we are addressed, but we are not always ready to listen. The signs are not extraordinary. Everything that happens to man is a unique address to him. The *I* is aware of the source of address, but no secret knowledge can reveal its sense, because it has never been stated before. A question is asked of man and wants an answer; but answers within general human science are only an escape. In the mutual address, the language contains no existing vocabulary, no system or program. The word communication cannot be catalogued, being a concretization of mutual contact.

Every sound is a new creation and only to be grasped by the listener, who must withstand this speech which only addresses him. These signs can be words or actions, but also silence or stammering, resulting in doing or non-doing. The situation which confronted the partner and which was unknown to him must not be built into the substance of his life. Then, his life is more than the sum total of moments; and the concrete happening he is entrusted with becomes his very own responsibility toward his part of human and divine communal life.

In Buber's *real* life, the *I*, therefore, only knows the world as a concreteness that is near at every moment. This concreteness is indivisible, incomparable, and looks at man only once. Every man is approached by the signs of address, which, meeting with a favorable response, could bring forth his creation. In this effort, man is walking the Between of a double path—toward the divine and toward the human simultaneously. If he wants to speak to man without including God, his word is not fulfilled; but if he wants to speak with God without including man, he is misdirecting his words.

The thought of man, Buber says in *Zwiesprache*, has something monologic, and he does not agree with Plato, who called thinking a "voiceless dialogue of the soul with itself." Buber argues that the "dialogue" is first proof and a reexamination of the developed thought, where one does no longer confront the origin. Not the empiric self is being addressed in the examination of the new concept, but the illusory self is addressed in a pseudo-dialogue. It is only in the desire for a dialogic approval by a partner that the genuine Thou of a dialogue arises. Confirmation of a thought, of its *I-ness*, Buber believes, can be reached only through a thinking power coming from the outside. Then the thought detaches itself from the illusion, and the concept becomes an object confronting the subject. Thus, in the primeval state of the thinking process the movement is directed toward a Thou. To Buber, the imagined Thou, as discussed in theoretical philosophy, is not sufficient because a thought has to be directed toward the physical concreteness of the other human being.

As even the individual thought process becomes confirmed only through the concreteness of the *Between* of I and Thou, man's role in life can be evaluated only in contact with others, and Buber arrives at the conclusion that the only criterion for existence is meaningful action within a community. Separatism out of protest as well as collectivism, are to him the enemies of a purposeful life. A social change is effective only when brought about by a community, so that it can become a communal reality. This goal can be reached only with the means growing out of a particular communal group. But it is doubtful to Buber that the members of many collective bodies still realize what the specific community is for which they are striving. Collectivity means, to him, individuals "packed" together; for he interprets real community to mean: not next-to-each-other but with-each-other of persons who, for the sake of a common ideal, a dynamic *across* that determines their goal, experience an I toward a Thou. Collectivity, Buber says, is built on organic shrinkage and dissipation of individual qualities of persons; community, on the other hand, is an organic entity and is built on the emphasis and increase of a common denominator by and for the members of this unit.

When a separatist group of men sing songs of freedom and mean only liberation of ties without responsibility, Buber says, their objective misinterprets authority. The individual members lack belongingness and participate with an *I* without giving their selves which—with proper inclination—could have meant their responsibility. Similarly, a member of a collectivist group has renounced his person and escaped the problem of involving his self. While the former replaces dialogue with monologue, the latter, in complete subordination, abandons even any monologic tendencies, and those who are in command of such groups do not make any attempt to reach their companions in dialogue. The dialogue and the monologue of these men are silent. They proceed not only without Thou, but also without I; those from the left want to abolish memory, and those from the right want to regulate it—separated enemies in a common abyss.

In Buber's *Dialogue*, there is neither a talented nor an untalented person, nor is there any differentiation of ability. Everyone has the same possibilities, since dialogue is no spiritual luxury. Through the *Between* of I and Thou, dialogue means the creativeness of a man whose only concern is his willingness to face his chance and to abandon a worn-out routine in favor of a reality when his moment has come. Buber emphasizes that nobody ever should believe that creation takes place in a special domain that is unrelated to the rest of life.

Man in dialogue lives by the desire to be confirmed and, at the same time, to confirm his fellow man. Language is the criterion and the proof of being man, and, in addressing the other, he treats words as he does objects. He distances them, neutralizes them in the world of *It*, to regain them in dialogue. The basis for this dialogue is the acceptance of the other-ness of the other, regardless of emotional, mental, and intellectual contrasts that may exist; for, says Buber, dialogue can take place only when the dialogic partner has been accepted unconditionally. In such dialogic conditions, without changing the partners, the substance of truth is shaped between them through their mutual influence. In this process, the relationship of each partner to truth is heightened because of the difference in relationship of the other to the same truth.

In his emphasis on man's meaningful existence which must be constantly reconsidered and reshaped in dialogic contact, Buber shows a certain resemblance to the philosophy of Jean-Paul Sartre. For Sartre, too, the rut of life—or decisionlessness—the *"en soi"* (in himself) is hell which man creates for himself. Only that man who lives *"pour soi"* (for himself), in constantly renewed decision, fulfills his existence. But Sartre says that, even though it takes the action of man to come to this decision, the action remains bound to the particularity of the man who practices it. Since his is not a response, but only a passive reaction, a reflex which is not oriented beyond the essence which each man creates for himself, this act remains basically concentrated on the individual that seeks no community with a partner. Buber, too, warns against lack of decision, sometimes called the "evil drive" because it is directionless, a turning in a whirl. But at the same time, in this "evil drive," in this disoriented passion, there is, for him, the potentiality of a renewal of a basically vital force if shaped into directness and *t'shuvah*. To Buber, this process exceeds existence, and, even though practiced by the individual through his fellow man in everyday life, transcends human boundaries.

With all his awareness of the decadence of our time, Buber never loses belief in man and in his elevation through the *Between* in encounter with other beings. He could never have uttered the words of resignation spoken by Meursault at the end of Camus' *l'Etranger*: "As if this great wrath had cleansed me of the evil, emptied me of hope, before this night that was heavy with signs and stars, I opened up for the first time to this tender indifference of the world."[7] Despite some aspect of hope for a better world in that "tender indifference," it is as if the Thou is felt and believed in, yet thought to be unattainable. Meursault, who, at the end of the book, wants to enter the world, and even craves for a "breakthrough," makes these final reflections: "For everything to be consummated, for me to feel alone, there was only left for me to wish that there would be many spectators on the day of my execution, and that they would receive me with cries of hatred."[8] This recognition of the whirling drive in man, that part of man that needs the direction, such as the "cries of hatred," could not have been Buber's conclusion, had he written the book. Camus stops here at the encounter and does not give the hero an opportunity to a "turning-in-renewal," his *t'shuvah*. Despite his "breakthrough," despite his new awareness of the relatedness of nature and man, Meursault, as a typical representative of modern man, lacks the directedness that could have come only from the bipolar encounter and exchange. Meursault answers before having been addressed.

CHAPTER 5

The I-Thou Relationship Transcending the Individual

I Fate and Freedom

FREE man's mortal life, in Buber's view, is swaying between Thou and It. A person enters the fringe of the sanctuary in his communication with Thou, knowing that having to leave this special realm again and again is the sense and direction of his life. At the threshold, his answer to his Thou forms itself always anew, but in the unholy land of his existence the spark has to prove itself. Man stands between the contrast of life and the spiritual power. In life, he is exposed to necessity; in the realm of the unknown to fate. Fate and freedom are tied to each other. In his freedom to realize his potentialities, man encounters fate. The specific action of the I is discovered while the secret in the movement of freedom is revealed. Fate, the counterpart of freedom, is not man's limitation; it complements his life. Carrying the spark of creativity, he returns to the It-world at his own free will; only at times of decadence he succumbs and is dominated by an It-world, because this It-world is not permeated by the Thou-world.

Buber points out that every important culture rests on an original encounter, on an answer to the Thou at the source, on an essential act of the spirit, as the example of Moses who brought God's message to the children of Israel might indicate. After such a historic episode, a specific version of this spiritual cosmos is created by subsequent generations, and man can build houses and temples, and he can form for himself the community of man. But only as long as he enters into the I-Thou relationship is he free and, therefore, creative. If a culture no longer has this constantly renewed relationship as its center, it becomes numb and an It-world. In such a decaying civilization, man carries the load of a dead "world-weight," and salvation can only come from a new substantiating encounter, from a "fate-decisive" answer of a man to his Thou. A whole culture then can either be replaced by another or rejuvenated within itself. The danger path is never the same, and, unless the existence of such a society is hampered by a dogma, a *turning-around* in the final phase is possible in what Buber considers a *breakthrough*. In this possibility of *t'shuvah* man is rejuvenated and transformed. The world of the Thou is never closed. Buber writes: "the one who walks toward it becomes aware of freedom," and "to become free from the belief in lack of freedom means to become free."[1]

Freedom means to believe in the reality of the duality of I and Thou. Man must not passively stand by and let an action happen; his own realization must be to him a question of life and death. Only a person living in dependency says: "Thou" and means "Thou that I can utilize." He has no designation, is incapable of sacrifice, and can never become concrete. The free man molds again and again a decision to walk toward his designation, but he will never force his decision in any way. Because he believes, he encounters. To illustrate this point, Buber speaks of the Brahman who tells of the competition between Gods and demons. The demons said: "To whom should we give our offerings," and placed them in their own mouth. The Gods, however, placed the offerings into each other's mouth.[2]

The purpose of mutual relationship is its own essence; through the touch of every Thou, Buber says, "a breath of eternal life touches us." Being in relationship means participating in reality or Being. All reality is mutual penetration in which the I participates without taking possession. If there were no participation, there would be no reality, or, with Buber: "Participation is the more complete the more immediacy there is in the touch of the Thou."[3] On the other hand, a self-centered person differentiates himself from others and moves away from Being. With this wrong emphasis upon his self, he can become fiction to others because he does not participate in reality and does not win any. He wants differentiation and possession in the It. Thus he remains two separate poles in one man. Then the person in man is truly lonely and leads an empty existence until, and if, he is addressed.

A searching human being, however, lives in a twosome I, the I-It and the I-Thou, and between the two poles history happens. History is man's fate which he has willed in his freedom of choice. It depends upon his true meaning in saying I, if a man identifies himself with the life of other men or if he entirely depends upon the significance of his own self.

Some great thinkers have considered the loneliness of man. Socrates believed in the reality of man, and to him man's solitude is never to be identified with abandonment or detachment from the surrounding world. To Goethe, solitude is pure intercourse with nature, which suggests its secrets to him without betraying them. He addresses the rose: "Therefore, it is you," whereby he is with nature in a reality entirely chosen by man, and to Goethe the friendship of the elements accompanies man into the lonely quietness of dying and becoming.

Buber sees two kinds of solitude in what he calls a pseudo-relationship: the solitude in which man turns away and detaches himself from the use and experience of the things which are necessary to initiate the act of relationship; this solitude lacks relationship. In the other type of solitude, man does not give up his connectedness and is immediately ready for God, because he wants to encounter God's reality with human reality. This solitude Buber considers as a process of purification which takes place before man enters the sanctum in self-examination. The first solitude is self-admiration, or a decadence of the spirit, while the second is self-annihilation. (In a true relationship, God embraces us and dwells in us; we can never possess Him in us.)

According to Buber, two extremes of an I-Thou relation of solitude have existed in the history of man; one in Jesus, the other in his counterpart, Napoleon. When Jesus says I he calls his Thou "Father" as a son only. In saying I, he means a holy I-Thou primal word which only for him rose to the Unlimited. Despite his awareness of a unique and greatly intensified I-Thou relationship, Jesus said to his fellow men: "Everyone can say Thou and is then I. Everyone can speak Father and is then Son. Reality remains."[4]

In complete contrast to Jesus is Napoleon, a so-called master of his age, who did not know the dimension of Thou. His was the demoniacal Thou of millions who answered with It instead of Thou. This third, demoniacal Thou stands between the arbitrary and the free, between the real person and the self-stressed being, and appears in fateful periods. He seems to stand in a cold fire. The relations with him established by his admirers are not reciprocated. He does not participate in reality, but men participate in him as a reality. He himself considers his I an It. He does not even say I but speaks of himself without subjectivity, declaring: "I am the clock which exists but does not know itself." He thus considers his I an unreality. He never understood his mission, says Buber, and his age misunderstood him. "Napoleon spoke the I without the power of relationship, but he spoke I as the I of fulfillment." In anyone else, such self-centered "objectivity" would be considered a self-contradiction. Buber thinks of

Napoleon as of a man who does not accept the a priori of relationship and does not allow the innate Thou to meet the encountering Thou. The encounter takes place within him and is not present, is not a relationship or a fluidum but a self-contradiction. Standing at the edge of life, he is unfulfilled and has an insane illusion of fulfillment.

II   *Man's Unity in Death and Life*

Buber, whose first concern is the existence of man, includes life as well as death in the totality of every living creature. In the last part of *Daniel*, the "Discourse by the Sea," he speaks of the interwoven elements of life and death which are the destiny and goal of man. Death, to Buber, is not an absurdity, as it is in modern French existentialism, but an antidote to life; for man goes slowly to his death from the moment he is born. Buber assumes an unusual role for death and tells the following story: Once there was death before existence, and its essence broke away in order to inhabit the forming power of two human bodies. From that time on, death always remained unfinished and needed for completion the human bodies to return to the realm of death. At the moment of human extinction, death completes itself and enters its Being, and man fulfills himself in death by going into it transformed. Life represents to Buber a maturing process, and death touches the sphere of divine action.

Buber's life-death cycle bears a breath of the poetic vision of Rilke—death being the dark side which, with the light of life, completes a circle—and of the quiet inwardness of Tshuang-Tse, who asks if life is a dream or a dream life. Buber sees the life-death enigma as a duality phenomenon, which reaches from birth to death and from death to birth; and the responsibility of man stands between these two poles. At every moment, a living being's experiences are filled with the mixture of the life-death continuity, and these experiences mix like man and woman and create his being. According to Buber, man in his existence stands simultaneously in stream and counterstream, and time is the only power leading to death.

Buber's essence of man, not too far removed from Sartre's "*pour soi*," has, however, none of Sartre's hopelessness of existence. Sartre, too, speaks of the choice and the decision of man during his existence, but his choice is limited to the existential forms surrounding man, and there is none of Buber's mutual penetration of the human and the divine during his existence. Therefore, to Buber, death is not "absurd," as it is to Sartre and later to Camus; instead, death is an integral part of life. Death, most of all, is not limited to a moment of cessation and transformation. Life creates Being, death receives and bears it. Both life and death exist as an element in each and make up the factual existence of man, whereby death is a constant movement toward change and shapes the phases of living. The body needs this action as the soul wants to complete itself in the union with the world. There is a fluidum between life and death and a union of the living and dead. Man experiences the world as a life-death duality; his task is to recognize and free this duality out of multiplicity and, in the end, to conquer this tension.

This duality has many faces; it is up to the individual to recognize it and to become its master. The two powers contained in duality go by different names—spirit and matter, form and matter, being and becoming, reason and will—but they all need the unification of their duality. In fusing the dual elements, Buber speaks of the tensions which must not be relieved but embraced and which cannot be found by following the wisdom of a given time. In a rare hour everyone has to find the simple path prepared just for him. He must accept the world of dualism and contradiction and not think of it as one of illusion that he can escape. Buber accepts neither a self-abandonment in asceticism nor a contemplation of the divine in pantheism. Man must neither conquer nor lose himself, but fulfill himself. Nature and ideas are not phenomena of a unified essence: they appear as dualism and tension. Therefore, neutrality cannot be unity.

Organizational attitudes and preconceived religious adherence are contrary to Buber's recommendation of individual search and fulfillment. His criticism of congregational decisions, born out of a sense of simplification, can be felt when he says: "If being [existence = life] of the world is one pole and not-being or becoming [movement = death] of the world is the other pole, and if the lived truth of the awakened is placed in the middle, that truth may mean salvation from suffering. But he who loses the polar ends and the ability of constantly being alarmed, has lost the soaring and singing of his life, the precious material of completed unity. . . . If I am the clapper of a bell, I want to become aware of my soul by touching in sound one of my walls, and not be resisting both. . . . As delightful to Him as is the silence of the Heaven, still more delightful to Him is the organ-playing of the Earth."[5]

When man attempts to attain unity in indifference instead of in recognition of the swaying of the pendula of duality, independence and not unity is reached. Man can fulfill himself in unity only in unifying his tensions and, in turn, in unifying the word's tensions through his achievement. One can perceive unity and become unaware of subject and object. Only in an existing contrast man can feel the *I*; the perceiving and the perceived form a unity, giving awareness of the *I*. The true *I*, Buber says, is like an ocean: neither ebb nor tide can say *I*, but the sea, containing the unity of ebb and tide, can say *I*.

Thus, according to Buber, unity can appear only in action; the sequence leading to this unity of action is always duality, tension, and task. With his inner polarity, man accepts the world's tension, and his soul experiences, simultaneously, both spontaneity and limitation, his own carrying and being carried, tranquillity and movement. At the moments of full polarity, man wants to act in unity and then only can he become *I*. The greater the tensions one is able to overcome the more *I*-like and the more truthful one acts. In experiencing freedom and dependency as one's own, the inner self produces the *I* whose functions are now both freedom and dependency. In the *I*'s belonging to the world unity is fulfilled and everyone's power of life is made eternal. The *I* of tension will be awakened in anyone who thus fulfills his unity of life and death.

III   *The Eternal Thou*

Buber speaks of three spheres in which the world relationship of man exists: life with nature, on the threshold of language; life with man, where language is formed; life with substance, without language, but language-creating. In these spheres, man looks toward the "seam of the Eternal Thou," listening to the breath of Thou, and it is up to him to create the Thou through relationship. He can take out of life with nature the physicalness when total encounter is to happen, when, as Buber says, the "gates are united to one gate of real life, and you do not know any more through which you have entered."[6]

Among the three spheres, life with man stands out because of the fundamental importance of the word. I and Thou do not only exist in relationship, but they also form their tie through speech and become full reality to the Thou of each partner, looking and being looked at, loving and being loved. To Buber, this relationship of man to man is the allegory of his relationship to God, and in God's answer the universe reveals itself as language.

Particularly in the third part of *Ich und Du*, Buber discusses the I-Thou relationship of the human-divine exchange and speaks of it as being extended lines of relationship that meet in the eternal Thou, because through every single Thou the eternal One is spoken to. The innate Thou becomes reality in the immediate relationship to the Thou that cannot become It, the Thou to whom only that particular moment can relate. Anyone addressing the Thou in prayer to God or through the Thou of his fellow creature is confident of his path; this faith then is confirmed in the encounter. The Thou confronts the *I*, but it is the responsibility of the *I* to establish the relationship.

Any true relationship to an essence includes, Buber says, all of man and is unique in the encounter because everything lives in the light of the divine Thou. Looking away from things of the world does not lead to God; neither does it help to glare at them. Only when seeing the word in God can one stand in His presence. Buber speaks of God as *the* totally different from, yet totally similar to, all living beings since He is *the* entirely present. Even though a secret, God is closer to man than his own *I*. Buber's outlook is reminiscent of the Hasidic sanctification of daily actions when he says: "When you go to the bottom of the life of things and restrictedness, you approach the indissoluble, when you dispute the life of things and of restrictedness, you approach nothingness; (only) when you sanctify life, you encounter the living God."[7]

Buber warns against God-seeking—even with all the wisdom collected in solitude and contemplation—because there is nothing where He is not. The path has to be taken, and man can only wish that it is the right one, and in the strength of his wish his striving is contained. Finding is not the end of the road, but its eternal midst. The Thou-sense in man is not fulfilled until it finds the eternal Thou.

"The relationship to God is more than a feeling," since feelings only accompany the actual relationship. In his heart, man knows that he needs God, but also that God needs him in all eternity. There would be no man if God did not need him. Man needs God in order to be, and God needs man in order to give meaning to his life. Thus the world is divine fate, and the fact that there is man, has a divine sense. Creation happens in us and to us; we subjugate ourselves to creation, participate in it, and contribute to it.

Buber considers the following two religious attitudes as incomplete: some men say that God goes into the I and the I stands in the divine One, and that, at the extreme moment, the speaking of Thou ceases because there would be no more duality. Others say that the claim of being within Himself as the divine One means that there is no speaking of Thou because there actually is no duality. The first interpretation expresses a belief in a complete union; the second, an identification of the human with the divine. Both are beyond Thou and I and cancel out any relationship. In the first belief, the Thou absorbs the I, and there is no longer an I-Thou because of the one-ness; the second thinks of itself as the I dissolved in the One's Self. Both religious leanings lack duality. Buber, on the other hand, claims that, if two become one in ecstasy, I and Thou are not fused, because any fusion is the result of the dynamics of relationship itself, which means an exaggeration of the act of relatedness. I and Thou are then forgotten. The other form of man's contemplation in God speaks of the fact that All-essence and self-essence are identical and that, therefore, there is no more speaking of Thou as the last reality. According to Buber, no teaching can give a definition of real Being, or else it would lower reality to an illusory world. When philosophies or religions try definitions or theories, they lose touch with the duality of existence, and man's meaning is clouded. Teaching "contemplation" in the true Being does not lead to lived reality, but to its "destruction," because of the absence of conscious-ness and memory. An insistence upon a non-duality, says Buber, does not formulate existence as unity; an inner reality of existence can only be measured in reciprocal action, where total man and all-embracing God illuminate each other in the united I and the unrestricted Thou.

To Buber, religious contemplation is the epitome of the It-language and can, admittedly, be experienced but not lived. As an example of an incomplete religious act, he discusses, in this connection, the teachings of Buddha. Buddha, the "fulfilled" and the "fulfiller," does not claim that there is unity or no unity. The explanation for this "lofty silence" theoretically means that a true fulfillment is beyond categories of thinking and stating; practically it means that such a revelation of unity would essentially be no foundation for a life of salvation. In the enigmatic world which man observes, Buddha does not pronounce: "Thus it is or thus it is not." Nor does he speak of "Being or non-Being," but he says: "Thus-and-other, Being and non-Being." Buddha does not want to create an opinion; he wants to teach the path. According to him, there is an unborn, uncreated, unformed Something, or else there would be no aim; for any path has a goal.

Buber admires Buddha and follows him thus far; he objects, however, to Buddha's aim which is the "abolition of suffering," that is, of death and life, or of becoming and perishing, in striving for salvation from the cycle of births. "No longer any return" would be the formula that eliminates the desire for existence and thus for constantly renewed rebirth. Buber does not want for man to try to determine the deadline and laws of his life and to escape his return, but instead, he should endeavor "in every existence to speak the eternal I of the mortal and the eternal Thou of the immortal." Buddha's decision in the "inner soul" renounces the ability of a relationship and fills man's soul with world and God. Buddha says: "I announce that in this ascetic body lives the world, the origin, and the dissolution of the world." Buber agrees that the world lives in man as illusion, just as the I lives in it as thing; but, for that very reason, the world is not in the I, and the I is not in it. World and *I* are drawn reciprocally into each other. This It-relationship is then cancelled by the Thou-relationship, which detaches man from the world, in order to unite him again with the world. Buber says: "I bear the sense of self in me, the world bears the sense of Being in it." Origin and dissolution of the world are neither in the I, nor outside of the I. They *are* not all together, but they *happen* at all times; and the happening depends on man's life, decision, work, and service. A man who truly goes toward the world, goes toward God and cannot be God-less. As Buber says: "God embraces the universe, but He is not it." Because of this "unspeakable truth" the *I* can say *Thou*; there is an *I* and a *Thou*, a dialogue, language, spirit whose primeval act is the word which is in eternity.

When an encounter happens, the incident of Thou between man and man is only brief. Their relationship does not weaken, but the actuality of its immediacy does. Every Thou is doomed to become a thing and to go into the It-world, so that it may receive new impetus in the future. Only one Thou never stops being Thou, and that is God. He who knows God also knows God-distance; there is never a "present-less-ness" of the divine power, but man creates the distance. Every relationship happens in a transition from immediacy to latency, giving awareness of the *I*. Latency that stretches between the *I* and God is only a catching-of-breath of actuality, in which the divine Thou remains present. The eternal is always in evidence; only our being human makes every happening an event in time and draws it into the It-world. The spirit penetrates again the It-world and brings about a change, when the I in *t'shuvah*—the turnabout—recognizes anew the divine Thou that has been withdrawn or has become obscured.

Buber thinks that one of the difficulties of modern man is to know when he is on the path that leads him to God. If philosophy claims that he only needs destroy his particular idols—products of art, science, money, and so on—and then his religious act will lead him automatically to God, it presupposes that the relationship of man to finite goods is the same as his relationship to God. But man's relationship to his particular values is directed toward the experience of an It, and the entrance to God is through a "Thou-speaking"-relationship. Having *possessed* these idols and wanting, in the same fashion to return to God not only changes man's aim but the type of motion. Buber regards man's simplification of his growth as a blasphemous "sacrifice to God on the same altar where the idols were overthrown." How can he whose idols are *possession* get to God if he is unable to speak Thou! He cannot serve two masters, nor one after the other. Life cannot be divided into a real relationship to God and an unreal I-It-relationship to the world. If a man applies his knowledge of the world as something to be used for his belief in God, his prayer, spoken in unrelatedness, is a process of relief and must fall upon the ears of emptiness; moreover, in this pretense of a relationship, such a man is truly God-less and not the atheist who, out of gloom, loneliness, and nostalgia speaks of the "name-less."

Many people today who are members of established religions depend upon rites or traditions but are incapable of establishing their own relationship to the divine Thou. Buber's man of God differs; for his doing is God-given command, an ethical obligation, and is to be considered an act of creation. What is "revelation" to this man who has personal religiousness is the moment of deepest encounter out of which he emerges differently from the way he entered it. This exchange is not an experience which excites the soul, but something happens to man that touches him as if in a breath or in profound struggle—as Jacob wrestled with the angel. As a result, man's essence has something added of which he know nothing before, and whose source he could not name.

The world of the Biblical revelation of God is: JHWH, "I am as the one I am."[8] Being is there; the eternal source of strength streams, the eternal touch is waiting, and the eternal voice sounds. Distinguished from any other Thou, the eternal Thou cannot become It because it is not measurable or immeasurable; it is not a sum total of qualities and cannot be found in or beyond the world. The eternal Thou cannot be thought or experienced, and the path to God can only be in directedness, dissolution of everything extraneous, and in renewal. The eternal Thou cannot say: *I* believe, therefore, *is.* To Buber, *He* is a metaphor, but not *Thou.*

Buber further believes that in any organized religion God is considered an It, because a belief concerned with time replaces any acts of relationship. Instead of a constantly renewed movement of substance, man finds rest and repose in a belief in It, certain that there is One who will not let anything happen to man. Instead of an approach in solitude, such a believer demands expansion in space for all his fellow believers who communally want to unite with God. To them, God has become an *object* of cult. The living prayer of speaking Thou in directness is lost because a personal prayer is suppressed by communal prayer and is replaced by organized contemplation.

The divine-human communion of relationship centers around an invisible altar. The ideal reciprocity in all God-man-relatedness is presented in God's revelation which is summoning, and man's answer is his mission. But in organized dependency of religions, man wants to deal with God instead of with the world. In placing a God-It into concreteness, he loses Thou. On the other hand, when man is ready to accomplish his *mission*, eternal revelation seizes the recipient and fuses with his essence. Buber believes that, as long as true prayer lives in man, his "religion" is alive. But religion degenerates in proportion to man's attempt to objectify his beliefs, to place his inner contacts into a world of It, when man attempts to speak Thou in temple rituals instead of in community-deduced solitude.

Two extremes will keep man from an exchange with Thou: subjectivism, which is spiritualization, and objectivism, which is objectivation of God. Subjectivism does not include the world, and objectivism destroys the truth, because the genuine word and its special meaning disintegrate. Buber says that times of an estrangement between *I* and world are times of disaster, until trembling occurs and "silence of preparation." In each eon, the disaster becomes more pronounced, and *t'shuvah* becomes more explosive. Because of this impact, theophany moves closer *between* the substances. In this mysterious history of man, the world-side of encounter is *t'shuvah*, its God-side is salvation.

In his *Nachwort* (Postscriptum) to *Ich und Du* (1957),[9] Buber defines the Eternal Thou. He says that one can only speak of God in His relationship to man in a paradox. One takes the concept from immanence and applies it to transcendence. God's designation as a Person is necessary to those who, like Buber, do not think of Him as a "principle." Buber means a God who, with revealing and redeeming acts, establishes immediacy of relationship with man and facilitates the immediacy of our relationship, that is, a mutuality as it exists otherwise between persons. This personification does not explain God's substance, but, Buber feels, it is permissible to speak of Him as *also*-being-a-person. To speak with Spinoza of God's many attributes, man knows—not as Spinoza says two—but, according to Buber, three: "spiritual-ness, natural-ness, personal-ness." From these three attributes of God are derived the human attributes, and man is capable of recognizing the quality of only one: personal-ness. Spinoza speaks of the contradiction in the concept of God as a "person" because, in addition to being self-sufficient, He must have His subjective character within the total of other self-reliant entities. To Buber, however, this necessity of contrasting a person with other independencies cannot apply to God, and his answer to this quasi-contradiction lies in the paradox-designation of God as an "Absolute Person," which means that God is one entity that cannot be reduced to a common denominator. God meets man as this Absolute Person and includes this Absolute-ness in His encounter with man. Man, therefore, in facing the divine Thou, does not have to turn away from any other I-Thou-relationship. He brings them with him in his confrontation and has them "transfigure before God's face."

To Buber, history happens in the clash between the unknown forces and the elements in time. Only when man is aware of his "timeliness," can God reveal Himself. There is no contrast between God's word and reality, and life is a joint effort of God and man. Every man can express his particular degree of belongingness in his very realization. All who realize themselves are equally close to God, and God realizes Himself according to everyone's kind. Man lives in action and influences existence with his decisions. Reality is the life of everyone in this apportionment of his timeliness, and true religion is the encounter of God and man, even though the mutuality between God and man can be proven as little as the existence of God. It is not a union, as in mysticism, or a separation, as in theology, where God is unapproachable. Buber's *encounter* is the living contact of I and Thou. The world is a "reality between God and man, in which reciprocity documents itself"; the object of a man's life is his creative message to God.

In man's response lies his responsibility toward the meaningfulness of his existence. The *I* that says *Thou* recognizes the I-Thou distinction, lets it exist, yet dissolves this difference in the supreme encounter. Buber says: "God *is*, and His Being is an eternal command to man," so that he brings forth *Being* in constant renewal. "God's side says: 'Being is,' man's side says: 'Being is to be effected.' " Reality of existence is at the same time man's fate, or, with Buber: "Greater than all miracle weaving at the edge of Being is to us the central reality of everyday's

Earth-hour, with a streak of sunlight upon a maple branch and the presentiment of the Eternal Thou."[10]

Buber considers man to a greater extent than the objects in the world. "If I turn to a man and out of the infinity of directional possibilities choose the one, if I face a human face and speak toward this man, something immortal happens." Out of the infinite possibilities Buber's "narrow bridge," the I and Thou, develops when the *I* has chosen. And if reciprocity is awakened, if the miracle is added that the same happens from the man across, the utmost for the sake of which the human world exists has been accomplished. Addressing God with Thou is only a continuation, an attempt of completion of what the human being is able to experience at every moment from man to man.

A momentary glimpse of eternal Being enters into human life at the supreme encounter, giving it a renewed impetus and sense before man falls back into dissociation, and renewed confrontation with the immense variety of manifestations, when, in trying to gain another step, he will again make his choice and decision for renewed directedness. It is a stepwise progression and progress, not dissimilar, in that respect, to the *Nirvana* of Buddha or the *Tao* of Lao-tse, but with two basic differences: (1) Buddhism and Taoism stress the reward for the man of superior ethics, represented in a final dissolution of repose after many phases of incompleteness; (2) the progression of man through various stages of existence is measured within him and for him, and Being and non-Being are exclusively considered for him. But to Buber, personal ethics is only one aspect of human existence, and man's gradual progress has to be adapted to the other man. Without the Between, without the fluidum of the dialogue with human and divine powers, the Being of the "eternal moment" can never be uncovered. All steps within the constantly renewed phases of directedness are taken in view of the Messianic age; yet there is no outlined conclusion, no reward for the single person; in eternal renewal there is an aim and a path, but no outlook for a specific Messianic Kingdom. Would there be such a goal, there would have to be a scheme to accomplish it, and with it, the individual encounter, its personal directedness and responsibility, resulting from the dialogic situation, would no longer exist. Any guidance, even of the divine power toward a specific conclusion, would eliminate the equal mutuality in the process of dialogue, destroy the life exchange, and reduce it to guidelines that are so convenient for followers of organized religions.

IV   *Ethos, Dogma, and Religion*

Already in his early book *Daniel*, Buber had been critical of modern religious practices. The dogma of organized religion was, to him, the cause for its spiritual decline; or, stating his concern even more drastically, he declared: "Every religiousness deteriorates into religion and Church when it tries to orient [man] in furnishing a complete view of this world and the world beyond, when it promises instead of danger, security."[11] Buber deplores man's attitude when he desires his own preservation instead of finding the courage for his own religious realization in order to fulfill himself.

If God's mystery is eternally revealed to a responsive man, he will realize God in all encounters. This readiness of man in realizing God-given acts is God's Kingdom. At every moment there is danger, eternal daring and beginning; and Buber speaks of a "holy insecurity" whose spirit is exemplified by the personality of Don Quixote, whom Buber considers the greatest poetic invention. Don Quixote not only runs danger but creates danger where it would not exist for others. Not to be afraid of danger—which Buber sees eliminated for man by religious dogmas—is to create entity out of all polar phenomena. Buber warns that "religion as a system is like blood that stops flowing." As morality can hide the face of man, religion can hide the face of God. In both, there is the danger of diminishing the dialogic power of a situation in an unpredictable, unique moment. Buber thinks that any dogma represents a danger because it immunizes man against revelation.

After having delineated the truly religious person as distinguished from the man who fails in his attempt to reach the superior Being through traditions and man-made dogmas, Buber tries in his book *Bilder von Gut und Böse* (Pictures of Good and Evil) to clarify the role of ethics in the life of religiously enlightened men as individuals and as members of their society. In order to arrive at the true meaning of an ethical conscience, Buber redefines the concepts of Good and Evil. He shows that good and evil in their anthropological reality are not two equal qualities placed at opposite poles. Rejecting this theory, one commonly defended in philosophy and religion, Buber speaks of good and evil as two structurally different elements. He is not concerned with finding a solution of the problem of evil but with a synthetic description of evil happenings. He tries to lead to the understanding that the battle against evil must begin in every man's soul. This individual struggle against evil must form the basis for ethical and sociological changes. Buber speaks of man who knows of chaos and creation—evil and good—wherever conceptual deliberations represent a gap between myth and reality. Good and evil happen; man experiences them in himself; but, being afraid of the taboos of the myths of his environment, he does not differentiate the manifestations of good and evil justly and tends to conceal the "voice of Lucifer" in his own life and, therefore, does not entirely face reality. On the other hand, the so-called ideal, paradisian state, which does not contain a trace of evil, has no content, and man is not asked to make any ethical decision. It was the "tree of Knowledge," commonly considered the symbol for the fall of man, which gave birth to ethics.

According to the Bible, man is free to accept or deny obedience. Overstepping a command is not reported as representing a choice between good and evil. After their fall, man and woman are not given the death penalty but are thrown into human mortality—the *knowledge* that man has to die. Having eaten the apple, the woman looks at the tree: she is aware not only of the tree's beauty but of the good taste of its fruit. Both eat, perhaps out of curiosity, the woman first, then the man as if in a dream. The event is a mixture of play and dream, ironically told. Both culprits are unaware of what they are doing; having no *knowledge*, they can only *act*. They do not *know* choice, since both good and evil are present. The tree represents the incision in their lives and the beginning of their awareness of choice, and is called *tree of knowledge* by God. The snake had promised them that they would become like God and recognize good and evil. It is only after the enticing speech of the snake that the woman *sees* the fruit of the tree and recognizes that it is "good for eating": but God says that it is "not good," that "man is alone" with his conscience. The negative adjective, "not good," was then translated as "evil."

Since contrasts in the Bible are always indicated either as acceptance or as refusal of something favorable or unfavorable, good or bad, without any scale or shadings, Buber says that there are three interpretations of this biblical passage: *seeing* the fruit means the acquisition of sexual desire despite the fact that both man and woman had already been created as sexually mature persons; recognition of "good" and "not good" means acquisition of moral conscience; and having acquired *knowledge* of good and evil means knowledge of the world, which consists of good and bad things.

It cannot be said that man owes knowledge as such to his eating of the fruit, or else the animals would not have appeared before ignorant man so that he might give names to them. They came to man as the bearer of the divine breath, that is, at that moment of creation when man was "filled with the knowledge of language." Knowledge of good and evil in biblical writing is but the knowledge of contrasts, a consciousness of the contrastedness which is latent in creation. Good and evil should, therefore, be compared to another contrasting pair of great importance in the Bible: nearness and distance. According to the Bible, it must be assumed that God knows of the contrast of Being and worldly manifestations which stems from His act of creation. He is above, yet near, and deals with the contrasting poles of *World* and *Being*—by leading them from chaos to creation—the essence of which is conveyed to man in dialogue. Thus, God deals with a contrast pair, with good and evil on an even scale.

Essentially different from these acts of God is the knowledge of man derived from eating the fruit. Unlike God, man cannot embrace the contrast. Good and evil, Yes-situation and No-situation of existence, enter man; but both situations cannot become present to him simultaneously. He *knows* only when he finds himself in a contrasting situation; he is aware of good only when he finds himself in evil. The process in his soul now becomes process in the world: his awareness of the existing contrasts, always latent in creation, breaks through into actual reality; for contrast becomes existent.

Nakedness and its recognition on the part of the first man and woman are not to be understood entirely sexually. Adam and Eve are shameful not only before each other but before God with each other. Basically, being clothed or unclothed has nothing to do with good and evil; only human *knowledge* of *contrast* brings about the *factum* of human relationship to good and evil. If God wanted to save man from the discordant elements of existence, Buber argues, man escaped God's will and guardianship and brought upon himself the awareness of contrasts of good and evil at the moment of his greatest nearness to God. Man's existence, from then on, unfolds in contrasts which always produce tension: woman, for example, must have unspeakable pain in bearing children, yet always want union in "one body," and the ultimate threat and contrast to man's existence are his knowledge of death.

As far as Buber is concerned, good and evil as such do not exist. It is man who, by his choice, gives concreteness to their latent qualities. His *decision* is the basis of all ethos. The post-paradisian copulation includes decision and knowledge, for Adam and Eve have learned about the contrasts in worldly existence. According to Buber, their sexual act is consummated because of their consciousness of contrast, and not—as religions interpret this act—as having chosen from two possibilities the evil or sin. Cain is born. The biblical incident of Cain's murder serves as an illuminating symbol of the ethical conduct of man. The short description of a fratricide is the first report of a crime. While Buber calls the act of Adam and Eve "pre-evil," the act of Cain is evil. God brought forth this firstborn, who becomes the first man to choose "not good" and who is the first murderer. The word "sin," now appearing for the first time, is probably the name of a demon besieging a soul. In this siege, man confronts the truest call to him of the God-Being, so that he may decide for the good and accept the direction toward the divine. In the biblical description, the quality of the soul of Cain is not called *good* or *un-good* but what is considered is his "good inclination" or its absence.

The lack of direction toward God in the dynamics of Cain's soul is threatened by a demon. The human domain which knows only contrast of good and evil is invaded by contrasts beyond the experience of man. Since man can only perceive the contrast introspectively in his knowledge of himself, he knows "evil" only when he knows it in himself. When God calls Cain, he does not try to search for this knowledge of himself and refuses to answer God; he also refuses to face the demon at the threshold and falls into his power. Cain's lack of decision is the decision of evil. He kills his brother, as Buber says, without motive, not knowing that beating might end in death. He kills in a whirl of decision-less-ness.

In exile, this expulsion from the God-reality—brought on by man—repeats itself perpetually. Because of man's indecision to choose and adapt objects confronting him, things not God become reality in his life. Buber speaks of this arbitrary reality as being man's doom. Even though man has *knowledge* of good and evil, only God can be superior to this contrastedness; because, in Buber's interpretation of the biblical passage, man manifests the chaos of possibilities which had been mastered in God's creation, while God objects to man and wants to "erase" him from the "face of the Earth."

Arbitrary reality, Buber says, is not innate, but invented by man for convenience's sake. As man faces the danger of turmoil in him, his *decision* is the basis of all ethos. The post-paradisian copulation includes decision and knowledge; for Adam and Eve have learned about the gave man good and evil to become his servants and to fulfill their service to him in "genuine collaboration." Without the evil drive man would not marry or bring forth children, build houses, or work since these acts compete with his fellow men. This drive is the yeast, placed by God into the soul, and without it "human dough does not rise." The drive itself is not "evil"; man makes it so whenever he separates it from its companion, the good drive, and makes the "servant" his idol. His task is not to destroy the evil drive but to unite it with the good. One has to assume that good and evil are essentially unequal. The evil drive represents passion, a power without which one cannot create; but, left to its own devices, it is direction-less. The good drive is pure direction toward God, which—as his only guideline—would take man out of his own realm. To unite both drives means to channel the direction-less potency of passion in one direction which makes it fit for love and service.

In other religious principles, too, good and evil appear as direction and directed-less-ness, as exemplified in the *Avesta* of Zarathustra who speaks of two moving principles, good and evil, presented as "twins." God before creation is not-yet-good; in creation, having become good. God struggles with the opposite power. God's primordial act is His *decision* within Himself, a choice between good and evil. Self-choice of the Good can only be good. Man, too, in his worldly struggle, is entitled to a choice between good and evil which always calls for renewed decision. To Zarathustra, everyone verifies himself in choice; doubt is *non-choice*, decision-less-ness from which stems all evil. Doubt in Being is evil; good is knowledge and belief in Being.

Buber thinks of ethics as being man's decision to unite the strength of the chaotic with the pure direction toward the divine. This decision is constantly redirected for the sake of the improvement of the individual in adaptation to the society he lives in. Buber's goal in existence is that man combine his ethical decision with his religious inclination. The question arises if under a religious impact the ethical domain in man can be separated from, be subordinated to, the rest of his life, or even be suspended. The symbol for the transition at the threshold of ethics and religion is the sacrifice of Isaac which is the focus of Kierkegaard's book, *Fear and Trembling*, which had a great influence on Buber's thinking about this particular problem.

The temptation of Abraham is interpreted by Kierkegaard as an example of teleological suspension of ethics, whereby an ethical obligation is suspended by a higher force. If God commands a man to kill his son, the immorality of the immoral act is suspended for the duration of this situation. The Evil per se has become the Good per se, because it pleases God. In place of a code generally adhered to by man, a different aim enters the personal relationship between God and the individual. Ethics thus have become relative, known values, and laws have been taken from their unconditional realm and have been made conditional. What has been a duty in the domain of ethics is no longer absolute when confronted with the absolute duty toward God. To Kierkegaard, man's fulfillment in duty is his way of satisfying God's will. Accordingly, God establishes the order of good and evil and breaks through whenever He desires; but only that man who has been chosen by God will be tested thusly. According to Kierkegaard, Abraham believed in God Who would not let him lose his son. Kierkegaard compares Abraham to Agamemnon, who prepares the sacrifice of Iphigenia. Agamemnon is the tragic hero who, within the limits of ethics, acts on behalf of his people. Abraham oversteps these boundaries, and in his transgression of ethics creates the paradox between ethics and religion. Abraham's dilemma is, then, that he dissolved this ethical inclination in his religious belief. To Kierkegaard, Abraham is lost because general ethical values are not valid to him at that important moment of his life, and he acts only for himself.

Buber feels that, in his account, Kierkegaard does not consider the important element of the hearing and listening which preceded Abraham's summons. God "tempts" Abraham. With the extreme demand for sacrifice He causes innermost dedication and complete intention for the act, making the relationship to God completely *real*, which is Buber's interpretation of man's ethical living. Then, between the readiness and the act, God is satisfied with the inclination and prevents the act. God asks nothing of Abraham, the chosen, except love and dialogue with Him. Therefore, He asks of him what is basically ethical.

In man's life, Buber does not see the possibility of a suspension of ethics because its practice is interwoven with the divine reality. Too quickly, man is ready, however, for a suspension of ethics, whereby it is questionable to Buber if the address to man is that of the Absolute or of something that "apes" the supreme Being. The Bible reports the divine voice reaching a single man to be the voice of a "floating silence," the voices of Moloch a roar. Today, man cannot easily distinguish between these voices which address him, and Buber uses the Abraham episode as a symbol for our own time which seems to be the age when the "roar," demanding the suspension of ethics fills the human world. Buber says that "apes" of the Absolute have always roamed the earth; people have always been asked to give up their "Isaac," but only a single man in his own self can know what is meant by Isaac. Buber believes that in the heart of man there are, and always have been, images of the Absolute; only since Nietzsche's slogan of "God is dead," the basic attitude in many men has changed. False absolutes have, for many members of society, wiped out the image of the real Absolute. These false absolutes pierce the "layer of ethics" and demand the sacrifice of man. When one asks "Why do you give up your dearest treasure, the genuineness of your person?," the answer is: "sacrifice has to be made, so that freedom, equality, and all other gifts can come to man." People think that fratricide will prepare the road to fraternity. Buber warns man to see through these false absolutes and to recognize that they are dangerous substitutes.

Buber addresses his warning to the daring man and not to those to whom becoming guilty means oversteppng the taboos, and to whom there is no other reality than the control by society. He is not concerned with what our society has made of good and evil and how man fits into man-made taboos. On the other hand, ethics of the individual should not be born out of the self-analysis of modern psychology which ties him to the remembrance of the past instead of the present before him. Buber believes in all that is concrete, reliable, unreduced and non-analyzed; and all memory, produced in favor of the lived present, is to be purified of omissions, additions, beautifications, and demonizations.

For anyone courageously facing this present, the accomplishment is enormous, because he will have tamed chaos into meaningful life. *Good* is the direction and what is done in it, and all strength and passion of evil enters the doing. The anthropological ethos, to Buber, is decision to directedness, originating in a revelation. This revelation then becomes human service, and the goal is creation. Without this freedom in dependency and creativity out of chaos, Buber sees no real existence for man.

CHAPTER 6

Buber's Ḥasidic Works

I Meaning of Ḥasidism in the Life of Buber

THROUGH his grandfather, Buber was in close contact with the *Midrashim*, the sagas and allegories of Bible interpretation, which constitute almost another Bible, the Bible of exile. As a youth, living in Galicia and vacationing in the Bukovina, he visited Sadagora, the seat of a dynasty of *Zaddikim* (wise men). These Jewish community leaders had a greater influence on the daily life than a rabbi. Buber had had many contacts with rabbis who led the members of a congregation on holidays and who, on those chosen days, explained the Bible and the place of a Jew in his tradition and his role within the congregation. But Buber had not previously encountered these *Zaddikim*, who led their groups as teachers, fathers, brothers, and friends through the distinguished moments as well as through the daily experiences and made everyone aware of the significance of each instant in life. For the first time, Buber witnessed a true practicing of religion, where every moment is sanctified and daily actions are full of devotion.

He now became very critical of the so-called productivity of the Diaspora Jews which, in the light of Ḥasidism, appeared to him to be only a semblance of existence that imitated the cultures of their adopted lands. Against this pseudo-Jewish life, Buber's Zionism, born not out of national-political but out of national-cultural motives, readopted Judaism which had found its most fruitful modern reinterpretation in Ḥasidism. In search of a meaningful Jewish culture, Buber, already as a young man, began to devote himself to the works written in the Hebrew language, and he rediscovered Baal-Shem-Tev, in whom he experienced the true Ḥasidic soul. What he recognized as being totally Jewish in Ḥasidic thoughts became to him the human spirit per se. This pervasively humane religiousness, fused with his childhood experiences of the *Zaddikim*, became his "promise" to the world and enveloped his writing, teaching, and life.

In concentrating on this aspect of Judaism, one of his greatest discoveries was Rabbi Nachman of Bratzlav, the Baal-Shem's great-grandson, whose tales were written down posthumously by one of his pupils. Some of them were fairy tales, reminiscent of those of the Orient; others were allegorizing stories, Buber began to translate them for an envisioned audience of children. But, since in translation these stories seemed distorted, he decided to tell them as if they came out of his own memory. After some futile attempts he became more confident, soon felt akin to Nachman's spirit, and decided to retell the legends of Baal-Shem-Tov in a similar manner. This intensive occupation with Jewish life awakened in him a new responsibility of his personal life and of his literary creation toward his contribution to the human cause; for Buber knew that man, with his being and doing, influences the fate of the world. He believed that the causality we can perceive is only a small sector of the incredibly manifold invisible influence of man upon every speck of his surroundings. Thus, every human action becomes the bearer of infinite responsibility. Some men are particularly well equipped and gifted to hold this responsibility, as is the *Zaddik* in the Ḥasidic communities. The naïve, the uneducated, the inexperienced, young and old seek his advice, and his words, with their immense responsibility, are "fate" to the individual and, therefore, to the living community.

Buber investigated the role of the Ḥasid (devout one, a member of communities without personal property) and found him mentioned in the history of Judaism in various meanings; first in the *Mishna* (traditional Jewish doctrine, as set down by the rabbis before the third century A.D.); then in 1700 referring to a group of ascetics going to the Holy Land in order to bring about the Messianic reign, and, finally, to the members of a religious movement half a century later, founded by Israel-ben-Elieser, the Baal-Shem-Tov (the Master of the good name). This latter group was not satisfied with preaching *one* doctrine of God, but advocated also a coexistence of men of all creeds on the basis of a divine truth they have in common.

Even though in his early years Buber became acquainted with only the last strain of this movement, he found enough genuine material to make it part of his own existence. In his research on the generations that had reached the epitome of the Ḥasidic spirit, he made their literature part of his own memory. This is probably why the allegories, experiences, tales, and utterances of wisdom channeled through him seem to breathe the freshness of life and do not have the flavor of translation or of retelling of a later period. This activity made Buber grow as a literary artist who, as the last sign of the Ḥasidic influence, wrote his only novel—or as he preferred calling it, chronicle—*Gog und Magog* (For the Sake of Heaven).

With the catastrophe of World War I, Buber's view of Ḥasidism changed. Now he knew even better that what mattered most was not teaching, but a way of life which was to give a commentary on teaching. This knowledge became important to his own fulfillment of life: not that he could adopt Ḥasidism itself, which sprang from a different Jewish tradition, but he tried to combine the Ḥasidic spirit with his world of dialogue. In recording the crude and disorderly Ḥasidic material, he found that he preferred the "legendary anecdote": "anecdote" because each communicates an event complete in itself; "legendary" because the anecdotes are based on the observations of witnesses. Thus, Buber could present reality and teaching combined, in the hope that its spiritual heritage might help rediscover humane goals and alleviate the crisis of modern man.

One of the important aspects of Ḥasidism is the desire to overcome the separation of the holy and the profane, in contrast to all systematic religions which had absorbed this separation, whose effects became schismatic in man's history. In modern life, a special domain has been instituted for religion and is perpetuated by state and society. Members of these religious communities then limit their religion to this specially elevated realm without including any religious meaning in their personal life or their public manifestations. In practicing Judaism, however, many acts in everyday life are introduced by words of blessing, permeated with spirit and hallowing the most prosaic doings. From here stems the view, particularly in Ḥasidism, that this "separation" is only temporary and will be totally dissolved in the Messianic world, where everything will be holy.

If Judaism is sometimes criticized for not knowing mercy, and for practicing self-sanctification and even instantaneous redemption, Buber says that Judaism stresses in reality the mystery of man's deed and God's mercy and the interrelationship of God and man. Buber warns that man should not try to take himself into his own hand, according to his own interpretation of his entire life span; for to be man means, to Buber, to be ready to meet a constantly renewed situation of choice. Sanctification of all acts simply indicates a process which is decision and beginning, and in Ḥasidic life this process knows no distinction between the domains of the holy and the profane.

II   *The Tasks of Ḥasidism*

The Ḥasidic movement grew in the eighteenth and nineteenth centuries in Poland and the Ukraine, where, since the expulsion of the Jews from Spain, there existed, for the first time, an independent Jewish culture. Jews were mostly village people, limited in knowledge, but fervent in belief and strong in their dream of God.

The Polish Jews were ready for a new kind of leadership. They did not need rabbis who gave them only instructions and sermons on the meaning of their teachings; they needed someone to tell them *how* to believe and *what* to do. The *Zaddik* helps his community of Ḥasidim in their entire lives, from their need of bread to the purification of their souls. The Ḥasid dances and is happy in the knowledge that his God participates in this joy. There are no secrets. Everything is open to all. The Ḥasid knows that in the Messianic hour all hopes and aspirations will be fulfilled. There will be nothing but existence into which *Thora* (Bible teaching and learning) has entered and where it has become life. In this community, there is no hierarchy in religious acceptance and in the acceptability of an act. No deed of man is too crude to reach out to God; or, as one *Zaddik* describes the fusion in himself of his inclination toward God and his awareness of the material surroundings, when he says that he "prays with the floor and the bench."

III   The Stories of the Ḥasidim *(1949)*

Buber used the very scant written Ḥasidic documents, reconstructed them according to legendary telling, and sometimes added related material to create a complete picture. His book, *The Stories of the Ḥasidim*, contains the legendary novellas and, still more commonly, the legendary anecdotes. A novella tells a fate that presents itself as a unique happening, whereas an anecdote tells a simple incident that throws light upon a whole life. The legendary anecdote is unique in the world of literature, because in one episode the sense of existence is to be recognized. Buber tries to eliminate all psychological ornamentation; he feels that the more direct the anecdote the better it fulfills its purpose.

Another category appearing in Buber's *Stories of the Ḥasidim* is the answer-aphorism: When a *Zaddik* is asked to explain a passage in the Bible, he answers with an aphorism. Even answers to unasked questions are contained in the aphorism. Nothing in Buber's book has to do with theory, and these folk tales retain their oral character. In Buber's selection, much available material was omitted, and he concentrated on those stories which give a characterization of the *Zaddik*. One might say that his book is a legendary reality. In the stories, the *Zaddikim*, the exalted persons, do not report about themselves but about what affected them as teachers, and their listeners are the congregation of Ḥasidim who try to apply these Ḥasidic teachings to the deeds of their own life.

In many religions the fervent ecstasy they create is unsuited for human experience and, therefore, is transplanted to another, more perfect world. Thus, the function of terrestrial life is a preparation for that better life. In Judaism, there has always existed a tendency to achieve human perfection not after death but during life on earth. The pure Messianic idea, however, could not provide this joy of existence, because hope for a future fulfillment does not create the immediacy of rapture. Even the Cabbalistic doctrine of metempsychosis, according to which everyone could select a soul to be identified with in Messianic times, did not sufficiently fulfill the life activities of the present persons. Complete balance of religion and human existence can only be achieved in a Messianic movement which penetrates life itself, and Buber sees in Ḥasidism the last successful interchange of man's physical and spiritual being.

In selecting and compiling Ḥasidic texts, Buber attempted to re-create the entity of life of his chosen persons rather than considering them as literary figures. Within the scope of this investigation, it will be necessary to eliminate large portions from Buber's material and to concentrate on the most outstanding figures of Ḥasidism; yet, in order to recapture the literary values, which Buber had placed into the realm of life itself, the material presented by these Ḥasidic authors must be brought back to the level where it can be called literature, that is, written artistic expression, once again.

IV *Baal-Shem-Tov and his Formulation of Ḥasidic Thoughts*

It is said of Elieser or Baal-Shem-Tov that his soul escaped when, at the hour of knowledge, all souls were in Adam, and it did not eat from the Tree of Knowledge. As a boy, Elieser had a way of leaving his teacher in order to be alone in the woods. He sang to the children whom he brought to school, and the "Heavens enjoyed the songs"[1] they heard every morning. Some legends speak of his simplicity, his poverty, modesty, and the performance of miracles, when, for example, an abyss was filled by a second mountain so that, unaware of the danger, he could continue walking. Some legends speak of his healing power, his wisdom, and the "light" of his teachings. They also tell of the trembling of wheat fields, water, and people during his prayers. He says to himself: "I am amazed, body, that you have not fallen apart in fear of your creator."[2] And he states: "When I attach my sense to God, I let my mouth speak what it will; for all words then are bound to their upper root."[3] Many legends stress his joy of dancing—reminiscent of the early Chinese poetry of Li-Tai-Po or Tu-Fu—stimulated by the drinking of wine. He believes that three things in life are to be acquired: love for God, love for Israel, and love for teaching; and, in order to reach this goal, one does not need "fasting," as other religious figures have pronounced before him.

The following allegory of the bird is Baal-Shem-Tov's praise of the rewarding effect produced by the united effort of the human spirit. A king wanted a bird perched high in a tree, and not having a ladder, he took advantage of the people around him. It took long to build the "living ladder." But those on the bottom lost their patience, and even with their slightest move, the "ladder" collapsed. Thus, Baal-Shem explains, not only are man's acts futile without the common effort of all, but also a prayer without the fervor of a community is lost. Against common attitudes, he gladly accepts in the community the simple-minded and the sinner who admits his failures, because Baal-Shem-Tov loved all creatures and believed them to be equal before God.

Unlike other thinkers, Baal-Shem-Tov's interpretation of knowledge is that we cannot *know* its last meaning. In this trap his two categories of men are caught: the one searches until he recognizes that he cannot know; the other gives up immediately because he knows that he cannot know. The one enters the palace of the king and looks at all the rooms only to learn that he cannot see the king; the other knows that he cannot meet the king and does not enter the palace. Baal-Shem's *knowledge* is not to be taken as a philosophical term, but in the transcendental sense of knowledge of God. Baal-Shem means the religious and the a-religious (non-thinking man), and turns against the one he considers a-religious because he gives up before he starts.

In more recent times, Franz Kafka carried the allegory even further in his *Trial* when he speaks of the man sitting at the closed door, waiting all his life to enter the house. Just before his end, he finds out that the door has been open all along. In Kafka, man is even further removed from the meaning of his knowledge than in Baal-Shem-Tov's category of the noninvolved person, because he is being guided entirely by fate, and thus is more a representative of our own time, of man who creates his own insipid fate for want of being a bystander, and whose inability of achievement stems from nondoing and nontrying.

According to Baal-Shem-Tov, a man who, in himself, accomplishes the union between thought and deed causes the union between God and His creation, where His spark, the *sheḥina*, lives. A union in God, however, would create a change in the Being of God, which is a contradiction. Therefore, the human influence amounts to a "floating paradox," and Baal-Shem says: "A perfect man is capable of accomplishing highest forms of uniting, even with his physical acts, such as eating, drinking, cohabitation. . . ."[4] The fervent one does not suddenly reach eternity but is climbing to it, step by step. In the "coming world"—never called a "Beyond"—Heaven of today is "Earth of tomorrow," and every world is more beautiful and purer than the one preceding it. Angels rest in God; they stand still, and it is the holy man who walks. This is why the holy man is above the angels. Rilke's angel, between man and God, quiet yet being a stimulus for human struggle, is superior to man; he makes man walk but is above him. In Buber's interpretation of Ḥasidism, man is superior.

V Man's Search for God

According to Buber's reevaluation of Judaism, a pious man seeks solitude and goes into an existence of self-inflicted isolation in order to bear the exile of *sheḥina*. As far as the Cabbala is concerned, the *sheḥina*, the presence of God that dwells inside every thing, is banished and roams about through infinity, separated from its Owner, and it will be united with Him in the hour of redemption. The ecstatic wanderer roams the world in search of the *sheḥina*, and he is a friend of God as, Buber says, a "stranger is friend of another stranger, because of their estrangement on Earth." When the moments of the *sheḥina* happen, they can be experienced in man and object.

Hitlahavut is the embrace of God without space and time; *avoda* is serving God in time and space. These are the poles between which the life of man pulsates. *Hitlahavut* is silent; *avoda* speaks: "What am I and what is my life that I want to sacrifice my blood and fire to Thee!"[5] Buber interprets *hitlahavut* as being as distant from *avoda* as is fulfillment from desire. And yet, *hitlahavut* streams out of *avoda*, as God-finding is the result of God-seeking. Between seeking and finding there is the tension of human life, and beyond his existence Buber speaks of the dual relationship of God and man. God is in man as He was in Chaos before the Creation, and man who collects himself and all his diversities serves his God. All doing in unitedness, and the spark of infinity in every deed, is *avoda*. In Hasidism, every deed bears both a good and an evil fruit, and God wants to be reached in all acts. There are two loves: the love of a man for a woman is private, and the love of brothers and sisters needs no seclusion; both loves, however, are directed toward God. Every movement of man's existence can be devotion and filled with power. To Buber, "man is a ladder, placed on Earth, and its top touches the sky, and all his gestures, doings, and speeches show traces in the upper world."[6]

The belief in the polarity in man's life, directed toward the divine force, is not only a reflection of Judaism but, in its stress on duality rather than synthesis, helped shape Buber's world of I and Thou. To him, the Thou of God permeates the world of It, to become Thou in the encounter which can be regarded as an embrace without space and time. The "sparks" for the encounter live, but they have to be directed to become the moments of Between of I and Thou.

These soul-sparks live in all that is, and the form of every thing is their prison. Man can bring about the salvation of the world with his *kavana*, his mystery of the soul; through any act he can make the *shehina* leave its concealment. Not the material of an action is important, but its *consecration.* Each person is surrounded by a natural domain of things whose sparks he is destined to free through his *kavana.*

For man to take the right road means creation, and the word is before all other forms. Language is a very important aspect of Jewish mysticism, and in Buber's thinking, words must be spoken as if Heaven were in them. "It is not as if you took the word in your mouth, but as if you entered the word." Buber speaks of three entities: world, soul, and God. They rise and unite, become word, and the words unite in God, because He rendered His soul to them. As *avoda* entered *hitlahavut*, so does *kavana.* Creating means being created, and being created is ecstasy. The artist, for example, undergoes changes while he is creating; thus he is being created as he is creating. If man wants creation in him, he must not be afraid to lose himself completely, abandon the elements of his previous self and walk with all his potentialities toward the unknown. And then God creates anew: holy creation through the pleasurable acts of man redeems the world.

Everything existing, in this Hasidic view, is unique and appears as in waves, which are new and never have been. This uniqueness represents the eternity of man and means his participation in time-less-ness, and man's obligation is to unfold his uniqueness and to help it purify itself until perfection is reached. Then when no other-ness retains power over man and he has completed his journey, he is redeemed and enters in God.

Man's unique life is proven in his life with others, because, according to Buber, completion can only happen through Thou and because of Thou, not only for man and his fellow man, but also for a member of the utopian socialism of his cultural Zionism, and for a coexistence of Jews and Arabs and all men. This feeling of being inseparable one from the other is to Buber the mystery of humility. Man is not to feel inferior but to feel the other's life himself, and himself in the others.

Buber accepts many aspects of Hasidism for his own interpretation of man's place in society. Everyone represents life, and to pronounce judgment on a person means to do so on oneself. Justice is to live with the other, and love for men is "memory of heavenly life." Many Hasidic legends speak of love for all creatures, and one is reminded of Saint Francis when it is said: "Love to all living is love to God, and it is higher than any service." One of the Hasid's primary goals is to "love more." Rabbi Rafael says: "If a man sees that his companion hates him, he should love him more; for the community of the living is the chariot of God's splendor, and where there is a crack in the chariot, one must fill it, and where there is so little love that it is detached at the joints, one must augment love on *his* side, to conquer the lack."[7] Love is the truth *between* creatures and is *in* God. For when one loves too little, the other will love more. This love seems even stronger than the Christian "Love thine enemy." Hasidic love expresses the mutuality: "When a man sings and cannot raise his voice, and another comes to help him and begins to sing, the former can again raise his voice."[8] On this mystery of union, on this reality of together-ness, Hasidism is based as on the conviction that mutual help is no virtue but the core of existence. Everyone has to be responsive as a total being, never out of pity, but out of love; and love means living *with* the other.

Baal-Shem-Tov establishes concreteness of life within the community. His only goal is man, and to him teaching man the *Thora* includes all contrast pairs: space-time, man-woman, God-idol, good-evil, holy-profane. Like Buber, he sees in everything the principle of polarity, and man's fate depends on making the correct distinction between the two elements of his contrast pair. The realm of the "end of the days" raises the question if the differentiation asked of man will be valid eternally. If he will have achieved his totality in Messianic days, there will be no more distinction. Good and evil will lose their distinguishing mark; the difference between holy and profane will be annulled. In Messianic perspective, the differentiation of the *Thora* are preliminary and transitory.

God is not infinite, but limitless. Infinite space and time are only limits with which God limits Himself creatively. A man who, in service, catches a small fragment of God's unity touches all of it. This contact is to the Ḥasid the mystery of God's unity. He believes that God daily renews His creation, or else his act of prayer would be stale. Buber speaks again of two kinds of love: one man loves the deeds and words of his smart son; the other loves his son, whatever he might do or speak. Thus it is with the love of God for man. As the first love is external, the second, even coming from a fool, is the love of God Himself.

Ḥasidic allegories about prayer show not—as is usually assumed—a spiritual permeation of things physical, but a physical penetration of the spirit. When Job says "In my flesh I shall see God," Ḥasidic interpretation links these words to physical procreation, because only the one who has desire and joy can succeed, and procreation can only take place with a "lively limb in joy and exuberance." It is also said that prayer is the bride who, after her wedding, has "all clothes taken from her when her friend embraces her," and the bodies can approach each other. In other references, God's two qualities, mercy and compassion, are called male, and judgment and limitation female; marriage is the symbol of the relationship between God and His world.

In his retelling of Ḥasidic stories in the German language, Buber emphasizes the importance of the word which, being the beginning of creation, continues the world through the relationship of God and man. *Sheḥina* is the word that entered into creation. The word comes from God who administers His creation. In this double form of One are contained thought and word in man who, as the servant of God, is only a vessel and whose words are worlds. Before a prayer, man must be ready to die in saying the prayer for the sake of *sheḥina*. Every word is a total form, and the Ḥasid has to enter into it with all his strength. It is only through God's mercy that man lives after a prayer, because he has given all his strength for the sake of *kavana.* There is no separation between man and God at the hour of teaching and prayer; however, this precondition of "nearness" to God does not necessarily mean an encounter with God. God is only near to that man who desires Him from a distance.

VI   *The Great Maggid*

To Dov Bär of Mesritch, the "great Maggid," spirit and truthfulness, were the only guidelines in a man's life. Knowledge is not knowledge if it has no soul, and to be admired for accumulated knowledge is, to him, punishment for a sin. More important than knowledge and wisdom in man is, as Buber emphasizes, his sharing it with his fellow man in dialogue. Prayer, the form of dialogue with God, can and must influence fate: "Man must scream to God and call Him Father until he becomes his Father."[9]

The "great Maggid" is using the amazing example of the thief as a symbol of the truly devoted, which fascinates Buber: there are people who never know how to open a door; yet every secret in the world will reveal itself with enough contemplation as symbolized in the thief who breaks open the lock. God loves the thief, because this is the man who breaks his heart for the sake of God, and his remarkable trends, or ten rules of service are: like a child, he is happy, desirous, never idle; he serves at night; he and his companions love each other; he dares his life for little, his prey means little, and he gives it for the least gain; he accepts beating and torture without concern; he loves his work and would not exchange it for any other.[10]

According to the "great Maggid," and akin to Buber, man can fulfill himself only in dialogue, which, with the least awareness of his I, changes to a monologue. In speaking, therefore, one should not feel oneself and should be nothing but an ear to hear what the world of the word speaks in him, and as soon as one begins to hear one's own speech, one must stop. To the "great Maggid," man's dialogic goal is not only the recognition of the otherness of the fellow man and the acceptance of full relationship, but also the tremendous power of the word that serves as the connecting link of the world between partners.

VII   *Rabbi Nachman*

The short book, *Rabbi Nachman von Bratzlav*, where Buber gives some further details, is one of his many references to Rabbi Nachman, because to him, Rabbi Nachman ben Ssimḥa (1772–1810) was one of the most fascinating and influential personalities, the poet among the *Zaddikim*, who wanted to give back "to the crown the old splendor," and who dreamed of the old days when the *Zaddik* was the soul of the people. Buber tells of Nachman, who, as a young married man, moved to the country, where he became enthralled with the beauty of nature and gave up his tendency for asceticism; for now he found God in all things. Rivers, fields, forests, everything in nature brought him closer to God, and he developed his service in nature, of which he often spoke to his pupils.

Exuberant like the young Goethe, Nachman wrote: "When man is deemed worthy to hear the songs of the grass, as each blade speaks its song to God, how beautiful and sweet is it to hear their singing! And, therefore, it feels good to serve God in their midst in lonely walks through the field between the growths of the Earth and to pour out his speech before God in truthfulness. All speech of the field then enters you and increases its strength. You drink with each breath the air of Paradise, and when you return home, the world is re-newed in your eyes."[11]

About his house, built of trees, Rabbi Nachman said: "If one fells a tree before its time, it is as if one had murdered a soul."[12] Later, back in the city, he wanted to renew teaching, not through books, but through life with his own people, and he asked in his prayers to "suffer the grief of Israel," particularly after his experiences in Palestine, which now became the goal of his life. When, upon his return from Jerusalem to Bratzlav, he and his congregation were the center of much animosity which followed him to the days of his death, he never defended himself but only said: "Whoever takes into his heart the reality that man dies every day—for he must give of himself every day a piece to death—how could he pass his days with quarrels!"[13]

More direct in his contact with his fellow man than Baal-Shem-Tov, Nachman taught that the world's importance is communication, language of understanding, and the link between man and man. Rabbi Nachman seems to anticipate Buber's writing when he says: "The word moves the air that moves the next, until it reaches man, who receives the world of his companion and receives his soul in it, and is awakened in it."[14]

Nachman likes the mutual exchange but does not care for the speech that merely reports a sense impression. To him, persons who have to announce what they see and cannot keep it for themselves are inferior to those who have their roots in the distance and can absorb for themselves what they see. Those latter are aware of the proper sequence, namely, the happening followed by the thought which, "dressed in clothes," becomes the word. The epitome of a dialogue is the relationship which reverts back, where the listener becomes speaker. "When I begin to speak to someone, I want to hear from *him* the supreme word."[15]

Rabbi Nachman was the *Zaddik* he meant to be, but the people whom he loved so much were not his; and, frequently, his short lyrical utterances are not bound to any specific environment and have a more universal character than the words of other Hasidic teachers. As many poets after him, he believed in man's death, which begins when he is born, and in man's rebirth, which is shaped according to the direction man gave his existence: "The world is like a circling dice. Man changes to angel, angel to man, head to foot, and foot to head."[16] He believed that, at the root, all is one, and, in the change and return of everything alive the salvation is decided. Man changes to other forms of existence, possibly to an angel being the higher, unknown static manifestation, but also back to a lower existence if the ethos of life warranted only this form—reminiscent of the Buddhist reincarnation for those who do not yet deserve *Nirvana*.

The mystery of Palestine is reawakened in Rabbi Nachman without any magical or mystic nimbus. He longs for the land itself, with an even greater intensity than can be felt in the legends of Baal-Shem. Nachman's voyage to Palestine was accomplished with great sacrifices, and to him the obstacles which one encounters on the way to, and in, the Holy Land, are very important. They are placed before the person who yearns to go there so that he can surmount them. Only then is he worthy to receive the holiness of the land. Palestine to Nachman is the primordial source of creation and of the coming world, because the land with all its marvels is the *shehina* itself and the land of the "resurrection of the dead." He believed that if one has not returned there so far, it is "because of our pride; the obstacle, therefore, is within ourselves."

Man has to die, so tradition says, because in his first sin the snake's temptation entered his power of imagination, and he cannot be redeemed except in physical death. In the right way of dying and with the proper burial place the impurity is dissolved, and in a new world a new body will arise. The absolute perfection in death and redemption, says Rabbi Nachman, is to be expected in the land of Israel, where the purification of man takes place through belief. When the children of Israel did not fulfill what was revealed to them, the holiness of the land sank into forgotten-ness, and since then exerts its influence out of this concealment. Nachman believed that Israel is a land of inheritance and that the holiness of the land can be conquered again through all who live there in simplicity of mind. This true wisdom, to Rabbi Nachman, was the meaning of Palestine.

His short life was not only filled with the best of the Ḥasidic spirit, but he raised its elements to a common human denominator. The poetic experience of nature of his first years was overshadowed by his yearning for the Holy Land later in life. And even though his influence was probably greatest in his spiritual, almost biblical attitude toward Palestine, the beauty and music of his language was never reached before or after him in Ḥasidic writing. It is through Buber's affectionate transliteration of Nachman's wisdom that an unknown Ḥasidic figure became an important commentator of one of the most recent manifestations of living Judaism.

VIII   The Ḥasidic Spirit in Conclusion

In delineating the Ḥasidic spirit, three of the great Ḥasidim—Baal-Shem-Tov, the "great Maggid," and Rabbi Nachman—might serve as examples for the diversity of attitude toward life and teaching. These men and numerous other members of the Ḥasidic movement played an important role in Buber's writing and life. Ḥasidism has continued into the twentieth century and nowadays shows traces in the life of Eastern Europeans in their own lands, as well as in Israel. During its most vital period, the *Zaddik* was the recognized authority, an almost holy man chosen by the Ḥasidim. Surrounded by his disciples, he taught, uttered words of wisdom, and especially influenced the life of his congregation through the example of his own life. Poverty, that is, lack of possession, even of intellect, to them was the most acceptable quality, and helping the poor was a daily task.

Beauty of nature and equality of all creatures found expression in many legends. But most of all, the exchange with God in the fervor of prayer, the self-abandonment in submersion, and the sanctification of every daily action became their life's fulfillment in view of Messianic times. There are innumerable ways which may lead to this end, and in pursuing this goal one must abandon all pride and self-assertion. To the Ḥasidim, asceticism is a wrong approach in trying to find God, because it is self-centered and excludes all dialogue. Love for God is exemplified in love for man, even for the enemy or the stranger. Israel of Konitz said in his prayer: "Lord of the world, I ask you to redeem Israel, and if you do not want [to do] so, redeem at least the Goyim' " (Gentiles). Praise of God and the holiness of everyday life is expressed in dance and word, the word, in its supreme form, being soundless, as dance is motion-less. This paradox is like nothing-ness before creation with the only promise of a return to Being that was before all manifestation of existence.

Ḥasidism means daily practicing of religion and its application to the worldly forms of existence, with the goal of a Messianic age. Ḥasidic Messianism is an ethical application of the medieval Cabbala, but this ethos does not follow accepted and expected conventions. The designation of good and evil follows its own laws. There is no evil per se, except in the lack of directedness. The "evil drive" is a positive force as long as it is directed in complete *turning* from a trodden path. The *sheḥina* can be found everywhere, and, as Rabbi Ssimḥa Bunam says, according to Buber, it can be "received in a house of prostitution."

CHAPTER 7

Buber's Ḥasidic Interpretation of Man's Beliefs

I   Ḥasidism and Other Religious Forms

BUBER frequently discusses the role of Ḥasidism as compared to world religions. In Christianity it is assumed that with Christ on earth God's reign has already begun; Messianism is but a "goal" in Ḥasidism, to which everyone contributes at every moment, and sanctification of any act happens as the unlimited ethos of the moment. In Ḥasidism, as in the traditions of religious law and the Cabbala, man is responsible for the fate of God in the world. God's soul, caught in the material world to be redeemed, is swaying between good and evil, time and unity, finitude and eternity. The Cabbala took over the idea of the "exiled God-soul" from Iranian religious beliefs, but changed the duality principle into the Jewish principle of unity. God's glory, the *shehina* in Judaism, comes from the necessity of a will, and the fate of the *shehina* is part of world creation. God limits Himself to the world because in the beginning He wanted to emphasize the importance of a relationship of love. Therefore, God let emanate the "other-ness," exemplified in man, that strives for entity. From Him come forth the spheres of separation, creation, and forming, the world of ideas, forms, and the realm of spirit, soul, and life. In all manifestations of life the universe is contained, "whose dwelling place is God whose seed is He." The world in space and time as it appears to our senses, is, therefore, the external garment of God.

In other religious teachings, the God-soul that was sent from above can be recalled. In Jewish teaching, however—particularly in Buber's interpretation—there is the double-directed relationship of man-I and God-Thou and their mutual encounter. Because of man's ability to choose, the world was created. Waiting for man's decisions are creatures and God. From man himself comes the impetus for redemption, and "God's mercy is the answer." The mystery of man lies in the fact that the fate of the world is based on its freedom.

Because of man's failures, the *shehina* is in exile, and in the history of Israel, the *shehina* wanders along with the people from exile to exile. To regain the *shehina* amounts, in Hasidism, to a combination of a cosmic and a historic concept. The ultimate aim is the coming of the Messiah, and, since everyone works toward a Messianic age according to his own capabilities, there can be no outlined plan—as it exists, for example, in the Cabbala. Hasidism seeks to "de-schematize" the mystery, so that every man may be responsible for his own goal within his particular realm and relatedness with his "meta-cosmic" responsibility, as long as the result of man's striving is subjugated to the constant effect upon the worlds he touches through his sanctification of all actions.

In redemption religions, such as Christianity or Buddhism, salvation is a fact, because the Messiah has come and established His reign on earth; in Judaism, redemption is an objective, because everyone contributes with his acts toward Messianism. In terms of time, the reign of God will be in the "absolute" future, as a timeless ideal—just how soon, is unimportant as long as man establishes the union of God and his *shehina* at any given moment. The Hasidic congregation is a social group striving for voluntary acts, and among the members the *Zaddikim* are the representatives of autonomous leadership. Their unifying force is their prayer, inspired by the intimate knowledge of a teaching tradition.

In Hasidism, ethical acts become religious acts. No longer isolated, they are between man and God; and, the Hasidim say, one cannot truly love God if he does not love man, and vice versa. When Kierkegaard says "One must deal with God only existentially," Hasidism says "One cannot existentially associate with God without existentially associating with man." If Rabbi Pinhas of Korez says "I prefer being pious to being smart, but I like goodness better than smartness and piousness," the ethical principle seemingly is placed above the religious. But in Hasidic tradition, "pious" means an isolated religious specialization, and the "good" man loves the world in trying to fulfill God's will in His creatures. Thus, Buber says, the way of the world leads to love of God in the universe, where one loves the sparks of God in one's fellow man. Since redemption depends on the unification of the human world, the genuine ethical deed is done in God.

Each human soul is thought unique and irreplaceable in Hasidism. God means with His creation an infinity of uniquenesses, where every one without exception, even the so-called evildoer, has his quality, his ability, a property not possessed by any other. If God wastes His love on the most evil, how can a man be as presumptuous as to administer his love for another with strict account as to honor and merit? Chinese wisdom says "Whoever brings himself into accord with the sense of Being, brings the world with him into accord"; Hasidism says "Your fellow man must be drawn into unity, where evil is transformed into good." In Buber's reinterpretatioon of Hasidism, loving the enemy is the epitome of the fusion of the ethical and the religious way of life.

In his article *A Presentation of Hasidism,* [1] Buber compares Hasidism with Zen-Buddhism. In Zen, mysticism is the annulment of the separation of I and Thou for the sake of the experience of entity. Zen, as well as Taoism, allows no thinking or direct utterances about transcendence, because "the *tao* that one can say is not the eternal *tao.*" Zen also rejects dialectic examination, even the contrast of *Samsara,* "stream of becoming," and *Nirvana,* the drying-up of the stream, because they are actually one. The Absolute cannot be comprehended out of general principles, but only out of the concrete content of human life. Zen does not advocate specific methods of contemplation, which are "dubious" means and unsuitable to reach the truth. It pronounces: "Everyone must find the heart of Buddha in his own heart" in communal life.

Zen monasteries are cooperative settlements of farmers. In doing work in physical-spiritual unity in "concrete reality," each member becomes capable of comprehending truth; this inner enlightenment, coming through work in Zen, in turn, leads to the greatest concentration of doing. In Hasidism, the key to truth is the imminent endeavor, and this key opens the gate to a life's fulfillment, provided that each act contains the conclusive message of that moment.

A Zen-teacher says: "If you want to see, look straight ahead into the thing; if you try to muse over it, you have already missed your aim." Truth, accordingly, is not found in man's knowledge, but through his existence. Another Zen-teacher, reproaching a pupil with having too much Zen, says: "When one speaks about Zen, nausea stirs in me." In both teachings, Zen and Hasidism, silence is honored. A *Zaddik* says "Learn to be silent so that you know how to speak," and a Zen-teacher says "Speech is slander."

In Zen, the road to the ultimate meaning of life, which is independent of man's physical state, is the relationship of man to himself, because a Buddha-quality is in each man, and he must bring it to the fore, without, however, ever pronouncing the name of Buddha or imagining his physical-ness. In Hasidism, God is the substance of man's prayer, but not his substance. Dialogue of God and man is not that of man with his soul, and man's essence cannot be identified with Being. Even the most personal Jewish mysticism always remembers the historic event of revelation, and God never stops being the God of Mount Sinai. The most personal teaching arises out of the connectedness with history, and each Jew experiences his religion as if he himself had confronted God at Mount Sinai. Buber says: "In Israel, all religion is history."

Tshuang-Tse asking about the difference between illusion and life, after his dream of being a butterfly, has no answer. A Zen pupil asking the same question is rewarded with a box on the ear and the cry: "Wake up!" Hasidism knows that life is not an illusion because the "Thora is the measure of reality." In Zen, all things are a symbol of the Absolute, which is superior to all concepts; in Hasidism, the things themselves are objects of religious penetration, because they are the dwelling place of the sparks—or exiles of God's essence which man is to free.

In Zen, only the "moment" has unconditioned reality, because it offers the possibility of inner enlightenment, and before this moment disappears, there is awareness of the dimension of time. But generally, Zen looks beyond time. Hasidism, however, sanctifies time: in Judaism time is tied to the revelation of the past, and, in its bond to redemption, points to the future. Both Zen and Hasidism stress the time-less-ness of the holy moment: but in Hasidism, when through man's deed the *shehina* is freed, a Messianic message has simultaneously been pronounced in two converging lines, the line of inner enlightenment and that of revelation, that of the moment beyond time and that of historical time.

Hasidism has a distinct strain of anti-asceticism. "Everything in and of men possesses sparks belonging to the roots of his soul that want to be lifted to their origin," says Baal-Shem. If, to him, eating can be holier than fasting, it is because fasting is only preparation and eating can be sanctification.[2] Man is a cosmic middleman destined to awaken a "holy reality" through his contact with things, as long as he does not deprive them of their thingly nature. The motto of Hasidic existence is that life in example is stronger than thought; the Hasidic belief is that God dwells in all of his creations, and the Hasidic eschatological concept is that because of man's desire to sanctify his acts and because of God's help in nearness, there is only One world.

II *Ḥasidism and the Modern World*

Since Ḥasidism overcomes the discrepancy between the holy and the
profane, Buber believes in its message for modern man. In his article,
"Ḥasidism and Occidental Man" (1956), Buber gives different explana-
tions for the problems of today's world: Marx explained this crisis with
the economic and technical development, psychoanalysts with the
individual and collective penetration of neuroses. Buber says, we should,
however, look beyond the symptoms and try to consider the totality of
man. As Adam is in every man, man tries to escape his responsibility by
using his existence as a "hiding apparatus." Repeated hiding gets him
more and more entangled in the wrongs of life, because "one cannot
escape the eye of God, but trying to hide before Him, he hides before
himself." Eventually, man will be confronted with the question of how
far he has ventured in the opposite direction. Like Adam, he will, in the
end; have to admit that he has hidden, and thus begin his true path.
Self-contemplation, correctly exercised, is the beginning of man's
meaningful life. With Rabbi Nachman, Buber suggests how to proceed
in finding one's path, namely, by using the rules of playing checker:
"One may not take two steps at a time, one may only walk forward,
and not turn back. And when one is on top, one may go where one
desires."

Since in Judaism every human soul is a useful link in God's creation
which, through man's word, is supposed to become God's empire, each
soul should purify itself, not for terrestrial happiness or for heavenly
bliss, but for the sake of the work that everyone is to do in God's
world. Man should forget himself as a person and become part of the
world. Ḥasidism negates actions toward personal salvation. The Here
and Now, where you stand is the beginning of the road. A Ḥasidic
story, as retold by Buber in *Tales of the Ḥasidim*, and using the
following allegory may serve as an illustration: A dream sends Eisik to
Prague to look for a treasure under a bridge. Because of the guard
stationed on the bridge, he does not dare search for it. In the end, he
musters enough courage and begins to dig. The guard, startled at this
peculiar action, is enlightened about the circumstances and mocks Eisik
for having traveled that far. If he, the guard, would follow his own
dream, he would have looked far away under a certain Eisik's stove for
a treasure. Eisik returns and finds the treasure which the soldier in
Prague had spoken about. This treasure is the "fulfillment of
existence," and the place to find is "where one stands." The daily
situation in the surroundings is this fulfillment of existence that is open

to everyone. Under everyone's stove a treasure is buried, and, says Buber, if man, in his search, misses his true mission, he misses the fulfillment of his existence.

III   *The Concept of Death*

Death, in Ḥasidic view, has different and contradictory aspects, but nowhere is there a suggestion of the abandonment of life for a world beyond, as entertained by Christianity. Instead, life is considered a gradual dying that includes a man's life span and begins when he is born. Fortunately, man was given the power of forgetfulness, or else he would be aware, at every moment of his life, that he is to die. Rabbi Bunamn expresses the difficulty of adjusting to this basic fact when he says: "All my life was only to learn how to die."

Expressing the modern view, Sartre and Camus say that death is absurd. Whenever death occurs, it means the interruption of existence. There is nothing in man that can prepare for the event. Death and life are, therefore, entirely separated, and despite all the protests of these authors, theirs is a belief in predestination, a fatalism that already penetrated the Greek drama, where no human action can influence man's fate.

These Ḥasidic thinkers who speak of death always include it as part of their life, either as the side of shade in the life-sun—Rilke's night-side of the circle life-death—or as life representing part of death in the gradual approach of the unimaginable event that could lead to another manifestation of existence. They consider important in their earthly existence the constant drive toward betterment and excellence of life.

Camus, in his symbol of Sisyphus,[3] comes close to the Ḥasidic view of renewal. The legend reports that the enchantment and punishment of Sisyphus was to roll a rock up a mountainside, "knowing" that it will in eternity roll back to the bottom, so that he will have to start again and again in the same effort. In the hands of Sartre, the same legend would have stressed the knowledge of the futile outcome of the endeavor, thus indicating the hopelessness of existence, and, therefore, in each new attempt of Sisyphus, there would always be the same disenchantment. There would be a renewed effort, but without the Ḥasidic "turning." In his interpretation, Camus comes very close to the Messianic ideas of Ḥasidism. Despite the fact that, in the legend, the renewed attempt is not a "renewal" of the person, the focus in Camus' retelling of the myth lies not on the effort of Sisyphus but on the moment of the descent of the rock. At that very instant, there is a glimpse of hope, and Sisyphus is really a happy man, because his renewed trial may ultimately contribute to the betterment of the world. As in the Hasidic Messianism, the ideal permeates the effort, because the coming of the Messiah is in the absolute future, where time and space no longer exist.

Sartre's freedom of choice cannot influence the absurdity of death, which thus remains within its own domain. Man's decision, his so-called freedom, remains bound to existence and has no aim beyond it. Unlike Sartre, Camus does not consider existence an unchanging manifestation. Camus' absurdity of death is the interruption of an existence that can contribute to the progress of mankind and the world. Death of an individual thus only prolongs the waiting for the Messiah. Camus differs, however, in one aspect from Hasidic thoughts, because to him death and existence are not one.

In complete contrast to Judaism, Christianity aims beyond man's furtive existence on earth which represents a step toward the *real* life of Christian interpretation, and which is beyond terrestrial existence. In Hasidism, the two elements of life and death are paradoxically paired. Death is part of life during existence, and despite the awareness of this fact, the Messianic ideal again and again renews this existence and, therefore, also renews its unknown event of death. Death may be at the beyond of a different corporeality, depending on the concentration of directedness that took place during the life span. The Christian conviction that the Messianic event has occurred, promises the individual no participation in a Messianic state. He is striving for a personal fulfillment that brings about a reward in the life beyond, depending on the quality of his human existence. In the Judaic view, however, the Messianic event is still an ideal of the future, expressed in Hasidism as a "dream" beyond space and time, unimaginable to the human spirit; yet there is a gradual contribution of each person as a member of a community—not as in Christianity for his own sake—and he "renews" himself without thinking of a "reward" or of a specific image of the Messianic age which eternally remains within the realm beyond human imagination.

References to the tragedy of death are rare in Hasidic thinking and writing. The stress is rather on the joy of living and on the utmost contribution of the individual, so that he can come closer to Messianic times, in a future that is limitless, and toward the coming of the Messiah, at the edge of time that is inconceivable.

IV   *Buber's Interpretation of Ḥasidism in Fiction*
Gog of the Land of Magog

During World War I, when visiting his son at the Polish front, Buber saw the towns which were the scene of the Ḥasidic folk tales and formed the core of his first visions of his chronicle *Gog und Magog* (For the Sake of Heaven) to become the epitome of his Ḥasidic writing; but he put aside the final writing after two unsuccessful attempts. When World War II created the atmosphere of danger surrounding the powers of false Messianism, the vision of a false messiah in the first part of the book, a Judaized version of Goebbels, gave the impetus for the final writing.

Buber did not want to summarize his personal ideas on Ḥasidism with this work; he had more objective purposes. He wanted to portray the *Zaddikim* who—in practical application of the Cabbala—tried to make Napoleon the "Ezechielian" Gog of the land Magog whose wars, as eschatological texts announce, were going to be followed by the coming of the Messiah. Other *Zaddikim* opposed these attempts, saying that salvation would come not through external gestures but through "turning" of total man. To both of these Ḥasidic representatives, the question whether fulfillment can come through magical procedures, as a result of the bloodshed of innocent people, or through inner change, was not a theoretical discussion but a problem of life and death. In this work, Buber did not want to retell legends, but, within the spirit of the tradition, establish the continuity of a "chronicle." He had to remain neutral in the telling of the two sides of the story, since they represent the discrepancy and cruel contrast inherent in actual existence.

The main theme of *Gog und Magog* is the conflict of the simple life of the "holy" Jew with the metaphysical outlook of the Seer of Lublin who tries to increase to the utmost the demoniacal forces active in the Napoleonic struggle of nations until these forces would shake the gates of Heaven and God would enter to redeem the world. The simple "Jew," however, does not deal with "world-historical Gog" from whose battles, which will transform the human world into chaos, Messiah is to rise; but he deals with the "dark Gog in our own breast." In *t'shuvah*, this "Gog" changes the direction of passion into a bright power and wants to bring about salvation. The "holy" Jew refers back to a call already heard within the prophecy of Israel: "First we must turn around, before God turns from the arousal of His wrath." And furthermore, he turns to the teaching of the inner dialectics of Talmudic times, according to which all eschatological possibilities have been exhausted. It is now up to man to "turn around."

Gog und Magog is in two parts and follows a chronological sequence, from the autumn of 1793 to the spring of 1809, and without dates in the hurried events of the conclusion. Two Hasidic forces are delineated against the evil force of Gog, or the anti-Messiah, who has been reincarnated in the person of Napoleon. Against this political backdrop, concluded with the fall of Napoleon in 1812, the principal figures are the Seer of Lublin, representative of those Hasidim who very realistically hope for the defeat of Napoleon, because, being announced as Gog in the land of Magog, his fall means the coming of the Messiah. Young Jacob Jizchak, called the "Jew," believes, however, that only the good acts of the individual in the community can produce the Messianic age. There is no animosity in the two *Zaddikim* who represent the dialectic principle within Hasidism, both expressing what the motto of the book contains: "The wars of Gog and Magog are led for the sake of God."

In one of his sermons, the Seer tells how evil came into the world. God knows good and evil in separation, man—after the interference of the snake—only in their mixture. God created evil so that His creatures could act against Him, as if there were no God. In the "desisting" of each is shown the strength of the divine power in him. If it were not for this power, there would be no good either. Parts of the "black fire" are sent into the world filling every thing; this black fire is afraid of the "coming of the light." But darkness can never suffocate light because light is constantly reborn. The hour will come when an immense flame of black fire will spread over the seventy peoples of the earth, sweep them along, and provoke a battle with God Himself. In the black fire's incarnation is Gog, and to him the Lord speaks that He will "divert" him and make him fall at the mountains of the land Israel. He will be felled by the one whose hand is fitted with the "sign of authority." God's act in the battles of Gog and Magog is reminiscent of the liberation of the Israelites from Egypt. His revelation after the victory of the people will be like the revelation to Israel at Mount Sinai. His "light of salvation will pour from darkness," because he hides in darkness and wears light like a "garment."

In the book, political events and conditions are sometimes discussed allegorically and serve as commentary to human behavior and belief, such as the following report: In the world of birds, there are two principal varieties, eagles and crows. Both are threatened by vultures who have already succeeded in chasing away the eagles, and are now endangering the lives of the crows. The crows are known for their totalitarian attitudes: they think that there are no non-crows in the bird world, that all birds are really disguised crows and have to be forced to reveal their true identity. A crow does not want to, and cannot, be alone. Leaving the flock, a crow dies because of the terror inspired by her solitude. Crows are totally dependent on the community in which they live. Eagles, on the other hand, strive for a community which to them, not having to live in it, is merely an ideal of existence. Transferred to the human world, both eagle and crow have the wrong approach to life: the eagle stands for the individual who insists upon facing his fate alone; the crows, for the masses who can only function in group action, as members of a collectivistic principle. The vulture represents the evil force Gog—Napoleon.

To the "Jew," it is not a question of eagle or crow: both flights or paths are eliminating the true relatedness. He is convinced that, before God, man stands alone in true reciprocity. All men are "erring souls of an only Father." We have to live toward a dialogic exchange. The "Jew" speaks against results which are calculated or wanted in prayer or magic. "If we *want* to bring forth salvation, we have already missed it." Perhaps one achieves the true goal at the moment when one does not try to think of it. "If we live from within, His breath is in us." Alone-ness happens in the awakening of a beautiful day; it is a lyrical self-expression. But a real prayer happens in the communion with one's fellow man and ought to be a community experience. On the other hand, a prayer must be delivered in the right spirit, or else one man can destroy what a hundred generations have built, when a prayer in community becomes mechanical, a process in which the mind is wandering and is absorbed in deviating inclinations.

The "Jew" who is concerned with the political crisis believes that God wilfully lets humanity sink deeper and deeper into misery. He speaks of times of greatest trouble which are times of God-darkness. Yet only then *t'shuvah*, which God expects of us, can take place, only then redemption can be man's hope. The "Jew" reminds his followers that redemption of the world does not mean "redemption of the good," but "evil from evil." If man would ever forget the contradiction in his existence which is there because of good and evil, he would wrestle with God and have become a follower of Satan.

According to the "Jew," a change for a better future of mankind can come about only when everyone battles with the contradiction within himself, with his *t'shuvah*; the Seer, on the other hand, predicts that Gog will fall at the mountains of Israel under the "blows of Heaven" and that help can come only from that part of Israel which has been preserved in foreign lands. He believes in the strength of the Jewry as a group having survived and having mutual ties in the Diaspora.

The Seer takes Napoleon's decline of power after the unsuccessful siege of Akko as the prelude to the coming of the Messiah, when the light will shine through the "shells" concealed in darkness. To foster this glorious event, the powers of darkness will have to overwhelm and to be victorious before the light germ deep down in the interior of darkness can be set in motion and can turn man's fate for the better. According to the Seer, complete purity must face limitless evil. Only then will God's light turn toward "light" and activate it; for light is only pure as long as it does not deal with itself.

The "Jew," however, is against anyone who wants to increase the fire of the coming danger. He warns only that *t'shuvah* will bring about the salvation of the world. God's world must be fulfilled with everyone's help. He warns that God does not want to unite with His *shehina* until men are ready to lead *shehina* to Him. Therefore, all eschatological calculations are wrong, and all efforts to hasten the coming of the Messiah are doomed to failure. Man must turn now and not depend on new wanderings of the soul to postpone his obligation. A decision must be made Now; no one has the right to increase evil. Before all Jews there is another salvation because "every leaf of the tree Israel" is waiting to be redeemed; no one can aid the spreading of salvation if life does not redeem life. The "Jew" is afraid that the Hasidic people will fade from the face of the earth, if, too anxious for the end to come, they miss fighting God's battle against the enemies of God, everyone in his own soul, in his own life, for the sake of all.

Toward the end of the book, Buber stresses that the news of Napoleon's complete defeat brought the Messianic tendencies among the Hasidim almost to a standstill. The dream about the defeat of evil had come true, but, despite the fall of Gog, life on earth resumed its normal pace, and the "prelude" turned out not to be the "decision of decisions." The Hasidim of both factions, those following the Seer and those listening to the wisdom of the "Jew," were numbed. Only very few began to understand and to see that one does not go to the Messiah; the Messiah comes to man. Perhaps the Messiah, so they hoped, will come when no one will call him any longer. The birth pain of the world will precede Gog, but the Messianic state after the fall of Gog will have to be prepared in "street, house, and heart." Wanting to feed the "heavenly fires with worldly materials" had been the Seer's mistake.

Similar to the teacher and his pupil in Hermann Hesse's *Narziß und Goldmund*; the Seer and the "Jew" are not opposed to each other but represent two opposite poles complementing each other. The Seer, wiser than his pupil, searches and, with the authority given to him as a *Zaddik*, demands the acceptance of his conclusions within his community. The "Jew" knows his own shortcomings and does not offer results except those that each one can effect within his own heart. There is no selfishness in him—despite the criticism that he neglected his family—but a complete devotion to all creatures and God, and the *t'shuvah* he wanted for himself and for his fellow men was to be the result of the battle with Gog in everyone's own breast. While others wanted to calculate their measure of reward in a Messianic age, he envisioned the redemption of the human soul for a better world. This is why Buber speaks of the resemblance of the "Jew" and Jesus the person, not the image of Jesus as created by Saint Paul. In both the "Jew" and Jesus, the relation to the world is not passive, but supreme faith in man's potential greatness is pronounced in their call to *t'shuvah*, the complete *turning* of man on a new path.

CHAPTER 8

Conclusion

BUBER turns toward the world, actively, in struggle, in dialogue, and not in silence. He seeks entity *in* the world, not behind or above it. This real entity must be "done," and he who wants to do it must first experience the tension of the world in his soul. Being in tension of spirit and matter, the soul experiences its own freedom and connectedness in a simultaneous process. Man accepts the tension of being and becoming, and the soul experiences its own tranquillity and motion, its own constancy and transformation. Thus, the world experiences its polarity from within, in man, who wants to achieve unity.

In Buber's wrestling for self-expression the word becomes more and more important. From the biblical beginning of time with the "word," language is the carrier of dialogue between man and man, and between man and God. The divine is announced through the human spirit and creates symbols until there is no symbol left and life itself becomes that symbol. God becomes real when one human extends his hands to another, and becomes the Thou to the I, which is Buber's dialogic principle. To him, "pure creation is pure speaking." God creates in speaking, and creatures stand in mystery of creation, of speaking; and all speaking is man's responding, his responsibility.

Buber avoids schemes and abstractions and tries to capture the essence of things in new, intimate words. Through too much use and abuse of words in ready-made formulae their power is diminished today. Language as it is only too frequently used for convenience's sake, serves as a quick schematization and a painless orientation in the world of experience, by pigeon-holing objects into the worn-out chain of causes and effects and coordinating them in a system of time and space.

Rejecting these modern simplifications, Buber speaks of a world of relation, in which the other confronts the *I* in his unique concreteness, where his *Thou* is present in the *I*. He visualizes the being he is confronted with and seeks out his relation to him. If a man or work of art speak to others completely, taking hold of an entire person, they are *Thou* to the *I*. The *I* then confronts them in their entity. This happens in a time-less moment, which is eternally re-created. But once lost, with the event of time entering, *Thou*, in whom a person found his *I*, becomes *It*, a remembrance, a link in history. The sphere for encounter is the "Between," and it may take place when least expected. Just as in his younger years the world of Ḥasidism determined Buber's characteristic views, he began, in maturity, more and more to add the Bible as a "living reality." Both of these sources became elements of his "religion of reality."

Buber felt that Israel's great contribution to humanity is her conception of God as a *reality* in saying Thou to God. Address and answer do not take the form of individualized prayer, nor is it in the exceptional state of a mystery cult, but is lived everyday. God in all concreteness is a speaker, and His creation is speech, an address once spoken to nothing-ness, in answer to which things occurred through their rise. Since then, the speech of creation is continuous in the life of all creatures, and the life of each is dialogue. The world is word, and Israel's message to all is that God can be addressed because He is addressing. Buber felt that this simple truth was changed not by Jesus, but by the followers of Christianity who learned to address Christ in God's place.

In Ḥasidism, "God is the place of the world." Because of God's dwelling in the world, it becomes "sacrament" in man's contact with it. Man's function in the world is to free, with his doing and non-doing, the sparks of God inherent in things and beings. The acceptance of God in all objects is the Ḥasidic message and represents the expansion of Israel's original task.

With no basic separation of the world and the soul of man, there is no evil. What we call evil is only the direction-less falling and striving of sparks in need of salvation. This passion, when properly directed, is truly good. But the worldly and the spiritual in man, not qualitatively separated, are his strength and direction.

Buber regards the division of life in God from life in the world as the "basic evil of all religion," which can be overcome only in "genuine concrete unity," as the *I* of the acting world-connected man faces his *Thou* in the presence of God. Buber says: "The defects of creatureness and the desire for its redemption are one." God dwells in creatureness and wants to redeem it, not just a man's soul, but the totality of the creature.

In Paradise, everything is like an open book to man, even the "tree of knowledge," but he is stunned by the mystery of a primordial lack which is the mystery of good and evil. Man in his frightened awareness does not rebel against God, he just does not opt for Him. As "direction-less" being he recognizes his limitation and accepts "good and evil," the "fruit picked and eaten." Man knows of direction-less-ness and of rare moments preceding the *t'shuvah*, which is decision. Giving direction through his decision is man's own motion, independence, and freedom. Man can "choose" or "reject" God; to fall also means to be able to rise. Seen from the other extreme, God can become destruction to the world, and in doing so, He can also effect its redemption. In the process of shaping the world, man is a co-deciding power and has freedom of participation. Not as an end in itself, this freedom of participation is the "creation" of man, and the world is its road.

The Jewish doctrine of redemption says: God is waiting for man in "history as it happens," and man in his lived moment is a link in creation and redemption. In active participation he stands in creation and salvation simultaneously, and God's Creation, His "word of prayer" is renewed every day. Jewish Messianism is not a unique, temporary event. The certainty of man's collaborating power connects the "time-end" with present life. The Messiah goes through the history of Jewish suffering in exile, where he is hidden as a "servant of God." Jesus as a concealed "servant of God" accepts "Messianity," and Buber considers him the "incomparably purest, most righteous, most gifted with real Messianic power." The Jewish world is unredeemed, but everyone's life is a "seed of redemption" and "God is the harvest."

Philosophy stresses cognition and reason; psychoanalysis speaks of our acts as determined by the subconscious. Buber believed that there should be a union of the two elements. Reason controls and gives direction to an undetermined power, and, based on many "hidden" factors, all human culture is selection, taming, control. Today's rationalism is not abstract but enters into life, wanting to act on the basis of a cognizance which was not attained. Within this dubious scheme, man is only seeking success. Buber, much influenced by Taoism, says: "Genuine working is not intrusion, nor exhaustion of power, but introversion, tranquillity-in-oneself, the mighty existence which, to be sure, does not bring historical success, the success that can be evaluated and registered in this epoch and in this language, but the effect, at first insignificant, even invisible, which continues throughout generations, and will not then be suddenly perceived as such, but it will have become a natural part of the life of humanity, so natural that one will hardly ask about the historical cause."

Philosophical-scientific perception deals with abstractions, in which subject and object are separated, and are, therefore, only artificial products of thinking. Science is built on the conviction that nothing beyond itself must be included in human considerations. In its thinking, the individual spheres of spirit and soul are independent or even said to be nonexistent. In a religious perception, on the other hand—including that of Buber—the individual, with all his essence, stands in a living relation which knows no separation and no abstraction from a concrete situation.

Buber's single man who becomes aware of *I* in the encounter with *Thou* is not related to the existential "single one" of Kierkegaard. While in Kierkegaard the "single one" may find his path to God, the person of Buber can go through the communal Thou as a "We" only in relation to the divine "Thou." Although much under the influence of past philosophers, Buber is chiefly concerned with man; and, despite his religious concern, he is no theologian but a "philosophical anthropologist." Hegel's dialectic was anti-anthropological; the socialism of Marx presupposed a matter-oriented view of the human world. Nietzsche was one of the first modern writers to dwell on man's problematic existence. His writing, replete with hints of the total destruction and deterioration facing modern man, culminated in his famous dictum: "God is dead." Misunderstood by both Heidegger and Sartre, this slogan led them to atheism, where all responsibility rests with man to create his own existence. To Buber, on the other hand, man, as an individual, has always been, and still is, ready for the realization of Thou, which was anticipated by the realization of We.

After the experience of World War II, Buber warned of the glorification of both individualization and collectivism, particularly of the latter, with its abandonment of one's own responsibility for the sake of a "collective spirit." Buber likes to find the middle way to these two extremes, the "narrow path," that is, the domain of the Between where *I* and *Thou* meet. This path is rocky and dangerous and leads "between the abyss on either side, without the security of expressible knowledge," but with the security of encounter in which both partners remain dedicated to each other.

In our technological age—the age of rebellion, dissolution of the family, and universal crises—the real relationship between man and man has suffered. Instead of aiming at principles, ideas, movements, which choose themselves as subject, our task ought to be the restoration of the bonds between man and man. If the *return* does not happen in the individual and in history, there is no future. The motto "Man needs God as much as God needs man" is Buber's ideal of a true human society, his "Utopian Socialism." Regardless of his religious upbringing, man must act with total responsibility for the benefit of all human beings as an end in itself and not as a means to an end. In Buber's view, the *Kibbuzim* of Israel approach this possibility of immediacy for a society living in togetherness. This model would be an ideal solution for world politics, which was led astray, as Buber says, by the "teachings of penetration and de-idealization of Marx and Freud." Today's mistrust is responsible for the hopelessness of the entire political world constellation, or, in Buber's words: "Each side has taken possession of the sunlight and has dipped the opposite side in night, and every side demands of you to decide between day and night."

Within each group, man must serve his God, and the political sphere must not demand the totality of the individual. Such a group must allow the individual to proclaim and attempt to solve an inner conflict at crucial moments of his life. Buber never wanted to advocate withdrawal from political obligations or for persons to be silent and to bow to the power that claims to act in the interest of the group, such as was shown by the horrifying example of Hitler-Germany, where the German people ignored the limits of what is political and, according to Buber, in the end took upon themselves "religious guilt" because of the mass destruction to which the majority did not object.

Buber attempted to define the phenomenon "man" out of man's dual relationship: consisting in the dialogue with God and facing his God Who, through His word, effects history. The theological element, fundamental in his thinking, is not derivative of tradition but a result of personal faith. He was bound to a philosophical language, which he made subservient to a perceived attitude and which is philosophical only to the extent that he can make his views communicable.

Buber wrote very few poems. Among them is a dedication to one of his Ḥasidic books. Its conclusion best sums up the meaning of man in his world of dialogue:[1]

> It is an end and yet has no end,
> For the eternal listens to Him and to us,
> As we sound out of Him, I and Thou.

Notes and References

Preface

1. Hasidism and other words in Hebrew or derived from Hebrew will appear in the text with a dot under the ḥ to imitate the sound, which is similar to the *ch* in German.

2. "Die armen Werte, die im Alltag darben/ Die unscheinbaren Worte, lieb' ich so./ Aus meinen Festen schenk' ich ihnen Farben,/ Da lächeln sie und werden langsam froh." Rainer M. Rilke, "Die armen Worte," in *Frühe Gedichte in Sämtliche Werke* I (Frankfurt: Insel, 1955), pp. 148-49.

Chapter One

1. Martin Buber, *Ein politischer Faktor*, 1917, in *Der Jude und sein Judentum* (Cologne: J. Melzer, 1963) pp. 501-4.

2. Leonhard Ragaz, *Weltreich, Religion und Gottesherrschaft* (Erlenbach-Zurich, 1923), reviewed by Martin Buber in "Religion und Gottesherrschaft," 1923, in *Nachlese* (Heidelberg: Lambert Schneider, 1965), pp. 102-6.

3. "Zweierlei Zionismus" (1948) in *Der Jude und sein Judentum* (Cologne, 1963), pp. 349-52.

4. *Der heilige Weg* (Frankfurt: Rütten und Leening, 1920), p. 85.

Chapter Two

1. "Ich sage zu dem, der mich hört: 'Es ist deine Erfahrung. Besinne dich auf sie, und worauf du dich nicht besinnen kannst, wage, es als Erfahrung zu erlangen.'" Martin Buber, "Aus einer philosophischen Rechenschaft" (1961) in *Werke* I (Heidelberg: Lambert Schneider, 1962), p. 1114.

2. *Ibid.*, p. 1116.

3. *Ibid.*, p. 1121.

4. "Das echte Gespräch und die Möglichkeit des Friedens" (1953) in *Nachlese* (Heidelberg, 1965), p. 220.

Chapter Three

1. Cited by Buber in "Zur Geschichte des dialogischen Prinzips" (1954) in *Werke* I (Heidelberg, 1962), p. 293.

2. *Ibid.*, p. 294.

3. Hermann Cohen, *Religion der Vernunft aus den Quellen des Judentums* (1919): cited by Buber, *ibid.*, p. 295.

4. ". . . hier, wo ich den Stock hielt, und dort, wo der Stab die Rinde traf. Scheinbar nur bei mir, fand ich dennoch dort, wo ich den Baum fand, mich selber." Martin Buber, *Daniel* in *Werke* I (Heidelberg: Lambert Schneider, 1962), p. 11.

5. "Mit all deiner gerichteten Kraft empfange den Baum, ergib dich ihm. Bis du seine Rinde wie deine Haut fühlst und das Abspringen eines Zweiges vom Stamm wie das Streben in deinen Muskeln; bis deine Füße wie Wurzel haften und tasten und—bis du in den weichen blauen Zapfen deine Kinder erkennst; ja wahrlich bis du verwandelt bist." *Ibid.*, p. 15.

6. "Um deine Richtung bildet sich ein Wesen, der Baum, daß du seine Einheit, die Einheit erfährst. Schon ist er aus der Erde des Raums in die Erde der Seele gepflanzt . . ." *Ibid.*, p. 15.

7. "So streift denn die Seele das Netz der Richtungen, das Netz des Raumes und der Zeit, der Ursachen und der Zwecke, der Subjekte und der Gegenstände, sie streift das Netz der Richtungen ab und nimmt nichts mit als die Magie ihrer Richtung. . . . Mächtig aber ist sie, die gerichtete Seele, da sie dem Wirbel entgegentritt, in den Wirbel eintritt." *Ibid.*, p. 17.

8. *Ibid.*, p. 22.

9. ". . . und nennen die Arche Weltanschauung, und verkleben nicht ihre Ritzen allein, sondern auch noch ihre Fenster mit Pech. Draußen aber sind die Gewässer der lebendigen Welt." *Ibid.*, p. 39.

10. "Solang der Himmel des *Du* über mir ausgespannt ist, kauern die Winde der Ursächlichkeit an meinen Fersen, und der Wirbel des Verhängnisses gerinnt." Martin Buber, *Ich und Du* (Berlin: Schocken, 1922), p. 16.

11. *Ibid.*, p. 22.

Chapter Four

1. Martin Buber, *Ich und Du* (Berlin, 1922), p. 17.

2. "Malerei verwandelt den Raum in Zeit, Musik die Zeit in Raum." Hugo von Hofmannsthal, *Buch der Freunde* (Frankfurt: Insel, 1965), p. 69.

3. "Die Menschen verlangen, daß ein Dichtwerk sie anspreche. . . . Das tun die höheren Werke der Kunst nicht, ebensowenig als die Natur sich mit den Menschen gemein macht; sie ist da und führt den Menschen über sich hinaus—wenn er gesammelt und bereit dazu ist." *Ibid.*, p. 69.

4. "Sein Herz sei die Nabe, in der die Speichen der Polaritäten zusammenlaufen; aber hier ist nicht Aufhebung, sondern Verbindung,

nicht Indifferenz, sondern Fruchtbarkeit." Martin Buber, *Daniel* (Leipzig, 1922), p. 62.

5. "Die Welt sagen: das schlägt die Regenbogenbrücke von Pol zu Pol." *Ibid.*, p. 62.

6. "... das Wort Gottes fährt vor meinen Augen nieder wie ein fallender Stern, von dessen Feuer der Meteorstein zeugen wird, ohne es mir aufleuchten zu machen, und ich selber kann nur das Licht bezeugen, nicht aber den Stein hervorholen und sagen: Das ist es." Martin Buber, *Zwiesprache* (Berlin, 1934), pp. 17-18.

7. "Comme si cette grande colère m'avait purgé du mal, vidé d'espoir, devant cette nuit, chargée de signes et d'étoiles, je m'ouvrais pour la première fois à la tendre indifférence du monde." Albert Camus, *L'Etranger*, ed. G. Brée and C. Lynes (New York: Appleton-Century-Crofts, 1955), p. 138.

8. "Pour que tout soit consommé, pour que je me sente moins seul, il me restait à souhaiter qu'il y ait beaucoup de spectateurs le jour de mon exécution et qu'ils m'accueillent avec des cris de haine." *Ibid.*, p. 138.

Chapter Five

1. "Und vom Glauben an die Unfreiheit frei werden heißt frei werden." *Ich und Du* (Berlin: Schocken, 1922), p. 70.

2. *Ibid.*, p. 73.

3. *Ibid.*, p. 75.

4. "... jeder kann Du sprechen und ist dann Ich, jeder kann Vater sprechen und ist dann Sohn, die Wirklichkeit bleibt." *Ibid.*, p. 80.

5. "Wenn etwa das Sein der Welt als das Ende und das Nichtsein oder Werden der Welt als das andere Ende bezeichnet und die gelebte Wahrheit des Erwachten in die Mitte gesetzt wird, so mag dies wohl die Erlösung vom Leid bedeuten; aber wer die Enden und das schwingende Leid verliert, hat den Flug und den Gesang seines Lebens, das edle Material der vollendeten Einheit verloren. ... Oder sei ich ein Glockenschwengel, so will ich meiner Seele inne werden, wenn ich tönend meiner Wände eine berühre, und nicht, wenn ich beiden widerstehe. ... Wie köstlich ihm das Schweigen des Himmels ist, köstlicher ist ihm das Orgelspiel der Erde." *Daniel* (Leipzig: Insel, 1922), pp. 143-44.

6. "Wenn aber die vollkommne Begegnung geschehen soll, sind die Pforten vereinigt zum Einen Tor des Wirklichen Lebens, und du weißt nicht mehr, durch welche du eingetreten bist." *Ich und Du* (Berlin: Schocken, 1922), pp. 118-19.

7. "Wenn du das Leben der Dinge und der Bedingtheit ergründest, kommst du an das Unauflösbare, wenn du das Leben der Dinge und der

Bedingtheit bestreitest, gerätst du vor das Nichts, wenn du es heiligst, begegnest du dem lebendigen Gott." *Ibid.*, p. 94.

8. Interpretative translation of one of the biblical names of God.

9. Martin Buber, "Nachwort" to *Ich und Du* in *Werke* I (Heidelberg: Schneider, 1962), 161-70.

10. "Aber größer als alle Rätselwege am Rande des Seins ist uns die zentrale Wirklichkeit der alltäglichen Erdenstunde, mit einem Streifen Sonne auf einem Ahornzweig und der Ahnung des ewigen Du." *Ich und Du* (Berlin: Schocken, 1922), p. 103.

11. "Jede Religiosität entartet zu Religion und Kirche, wenn sie zu orientieren beginnt; wenn sie . . . eine Übersicht des Dies- und Jenseits gibt . . ., und statt der Gefahr die Sicherheit verspricht." *Daniel* (Leipzig: Insel, 1922), p. 71.

Chapter Six

1. Martin Buber, *Die Erzählungen der Chassidim* (1949) in *Werke* III (Heidelberg: Schneider, 1963), 153.

2. "Ich wundere mich, Leib, daß du noch nicht zerbröckelt bist aus Furcht vor deinem Schöpfer." *Ibid.*, p. 166.

3. "Wenn der Mensch sich an Gott schließt, kann er seinen Mund reden lassen, was er reden mag, und sein Ohr hören lassen, was es hören mag, und er wird die Dinge binden an ihre obere Wurzel." Martin Buber, *Vom Leben der Chassidim* (1920) in *Werke* III (Heidelberg: Schneider, 1963), p. 21.

4. " 'Der vollkommene Mensch,' sagt der Baalschem, 'vermag höchste Einungen zu vollziehen' (d.h. Gott mit seiner im Exil der Welt weilenden Schechina zu vereinigen), 'sogar mit seinen leiblichen Handlungen, so Essen, Trinken, Beischlaf. . . .' " *Zur Darstellung des Chassidismus* (1963) in *Werke* III (Heidelberg: Schneider, 1963), 979.

5. *Vom Leben der Chassidim* (1920) in *Werke* III (Heidelberg: Schneider, 1963), p. 26.

6. "Der Mensch ist eine Leiter, gestellt auf die Erde, und ihr Haupt rührt an den Himmel. Und alle seine Gebärden und Geschäfte und Reden ziehen Spuren in der oberen Welt." *Ibid.*, p. 28.

7. " 'Wenn ein Mensch sieht, daß sein Gefährte ihn haßt, soll er ihn mehr lieben. Denn die Gemeinschaft der Lebendigen ist der Wagen der er Gottesherrlichkeit, und wo ein Riß im Wagen ist, muß man ihn füllen, und wo der Liebe wenig ist, daß die Fügung sich löst, muß man Liebe mehren auf *seiner* Seite, den Mangel zu zwingen.' " *Ibid.*, p. 43.

8. " 'Wenn ein Mensch singt und kann die Stimme nicht erheben, und einer kommt ihm zu helfen und hebt an zu singen, dann kann auch jener wieder die Stimme erheben.' " *Ibid.*, p. 44.

9. " 'Der Mensch muß zu Gott schreien und ihn Vater nennen, bis er

sein Vater wird.' " *Die Erzählungen der Chassidim* (1949) in *Werke* III (Heidelberg: Schneider, 1963), p. 221.

10. *Der große Maggid und seine Nachfolge* (Frankfurt: Rütten und Loening, 1922), p. 11.

11. " 'Wenn der Mensch gewürdigt wird,' redete er zu ihnen, 'die Gesänge der Kräuter zu vernehmen, wie jedes Kraut sein Lied zu Gott spricht, wie schön und süß ist es, ihr Singen zu hören! Und daher tut es gar gut, in ihrer Mitte Gott zu dienen in einsamem Wandeln über das Feld hin zwischen den Gewächsen der Erde und seine Rede auszuschütten vor Gott in Wahrhaftigkeit. Alle Rede des Feldes geht dann in deine ein und steigert ihre Kraft. Du trinkst mit jedem Atemzug die Luft des Paradieses, und kehrst du heim, ist die Welt erneuert in deinen Augen.' " *Rabbi Nachman von Bratzlaw* (1906) in *Werke* III (Heidelberg: Schneider, 1963), p. 899.

12. " 'Denn wenn man einen Baum vor seiner Zeit abhaut, ist es, als hätte man eine Seele gemordet.' " *Ibid.*, p. 900.

13. " 'Aber wer in sein Herz die Wirklichkeit aufnimmt, daß der Mensch an jedem Tage stirbt, denn er muß jeden Tag ein Stück von sich seinem Tode abgeben, wie soll der noch seine Tage mit Streit verbringen können.' " *Ibid.*, p. 901.

14. " 'Das Wort bewegt eine Luft und diese die nächste, bis es zum Menschen gelangt, der empfängt das Wort des Genossen und empfängt seine Seele darin und wird darin erweckt.' " *Ibid.*, p. 902.

15. " 'Wenn ich mit einem zu reden beginne, will ich von *ihm* die höchsten Worte hören.' " *Ibid.*, p. 903.

16. "Die Welt ist wie ein kreisender Würfel, und alles kehrt sich, und es wandelt sich der Mensch zum Engel und der Engel zum Menschen und das Haupt zum Fuß und der Fuß zum Haupt. . . ." *Ibid.*, p. 106.

Chapter Seven

1. "Noch einiges zur Darstellung des Chassidismus" in *Werke* III (Heidelberg: Schneider, 1963), pp. 991-98.

2. "Auch in der Speise wohnen heilige Funken, und das Essen kann daher heiliger sein als das Fasten." "Der Chassidismus und der abendländische Mensch" in *Werke* III (Heidelberg: Schneider, 1963), p. 941f.

3. Albert Camus, "Le Mythe de Sisyphe" in *De l'Envers et l'Endroit a l'Exile et le Royaume*, ed. G. Brée (New York: Dell, 1963), pp. 63-73.

Chapter Eight

1. "Es ist ein Ende und hat doch kein Ende,/ Denn Ewiges hört ihm und hört uns zu,/ Wie wir aus ihm ertönen, ich und du." Martin Buber, "Weißt du es noch? . . ." in *Nachlese* (Heidelberg: Schneider, 1965), p. 26.

Selected Bibliography

PRIMARY SOURCES

The complete works of Martin Buber, published in Munich by the Kösel-Verlag and in Heidelberg by Lambert Schneider in. 1962-63, contain 3 volumes:

I. *Schriften zur Philosophie*
II. *Schriften zur Bibel*
III. *Schriften zum Chassidismus.*

An additional volume, published in Cologne by Joseph Melzer in 1963, is entitled: *Der Jude und sein Judentum.* The short volume, *Nachlese*, published in 1965, shortly before Martin Buber's death, by Lambert Schneider, contains articles, speeches, and poems. In these primary sources, only key works which played a role in the preparation of this study are given. They appear in each section in chronological order.

1. Philosophy

Reden und Gleichnisse des Tschuang-Tse (Leipzig, Insel, 1910). Out of print.

Daniel. Gespräche von der Verwirklichung (Leipzig: Insel, 1922).

Ich und Du (Leipzig: Insel, 1922).

Zwiesprache (Berlin: Schocken, 1932; 2nd rev. ed. 1934).

Die Frage an den Einzelnen (Berlin, Schocken, 1936).

Gottesfinsternis. Betrachtungen zur Beziehung zwischen Religion und Philosophie in *Werke* I (Munich: Kösel and Heidelberg: Lambert Schneider, 1962), 503-603. *Eclipse of God. Studies in the Relation between Religion and Philosophy* (New York: Harper & Row, Harper Torchbook, 1957; 6th printing, 1965).

Bilder von Gut und Böse (Cologne: Jacob Hegner, 1952).

Pfade in Utopia (Heidelberg: Lambert Schneider, 1952).

Beiträge zu einer philosophischen Anthropologie in *Werke* I (Heidelberg: Lambert Schneider, 1962), pp. 409-502.

Nachlese (Heidelberg: Lambert Schneider, 1965).

2. Judaism
Der heilige Weg (Frankfurt: Rütten & Loening, 1920).
Königtum Gottes (Berlin: Schocken, 1932).
Kampf um Israel (Berlin: Schocken, 1933).
Moses (Heidelberg: Lambert Schneider, 1952).
Elija. Ein Mysterienspiel. (Heidelberg: Lambert Schneider, 1963).
Der Jude und sein Judentum (Cologne: J. Melzer, 1963).

3. Hasidism
Die Geschichten des Rabbi Nachman (Frankfurt: Rütten & Loening, 1906).
Die Legende des Baal Schem (Frankfurt: Rütten & Loening, 1908).
Der große Maggid und seine Nachfolge (Frankfurt: Rütten & Loening, 1922).
Des Rabbi Israel ben Elieser genannt Baal-Schem-Tow, das ist Meister des guten Namen im Umgang mit Gott (Berlin: Schocken, 1935).
Die Erzählungen der Chassidim (Zurich: Manesse, 1949).
Die chassidische Botschaft (Heidelberg: Lambert Schneider, 1952).
Gog und Magog. Eine Chronik in *Werke* II (Munich: Kösel; Heidelberg: Lambert Schneider, 1963), pp. 999-1261.

4. Articles, Essays, and Speeches
Nachwort. Reden und Gleichnisse des Tschuang-Tse (Leipzig: Insel, 1910), pp. 82-122.
Mein Weg zum Chassidismus (1917) in *Werke* III (Heidelberg: Schneider, 1963, pp. 959-73.
Drei Reden über das Judentum (Frankfurt: Rütten & Loening, 1923).
Gandhi, die Politik und wir (1930) in *Werke* I (Heidelberg: Schneider, 1962), pp. 1979-87.
Zu Bergsons Begriff der Intuition in *Werke* I (Munich: Kösel and Heidelberg: Schneider, 1962), pp. 1071-78.
Christus, Chassidismus und Gnosis (1954) in *Werke* III (Heidelberg: Schneider, 1963), pp. 949-58.
Zur Geschichte des dialogischen Prinzips (1954) in *Werke* II (Heidelberg: Schneider, 1963), pp. 291-305.
Chassidsmus und der abendländische Mensch (1956) in *Werke* III (Heidelberg: Schneider, 1963), pp. 993-47.
Der Weg des Menschen nach der chassidischen Lehre (1960) *ibid.*, pp. 713-38.
Zur Darstellung des Chassidismus. Ibid., pp. 975-88.
Noch einiges zur Darstellung des Chassidismus. Ibid., pp. 989-98.

SECONDARY SOURCES

COHEN, ARTHUR A. *Martin Buber* (London: Bower & Bower, 1957).

DIAMOND, MALCOLM L. *Martin Buber—Jewish Existentialist* (New York: Oxford University Press, 1960).

FRIEDMAN, MAURICE. Martin Buber. *The Life of Dialogue* (Chicago: University of Chicago Press, 1955).

HERBERG, WILL. *The Writings of Martin Buber* (Cleveland and New York: The World Publishing Co. Meridian Books, 1956, 8th printing, 1965). A short Buber reader.

HODES, AUBREY. *Martin Buber. An Intimate Portrait* (New York: The Viking Press, 1971).

KOHN, HANS. *Martin Buber. Sein Werk und seine Zeit* (Cologne: J. Melzer, 1961). A reprint of a work originally published in 1930 with concluding remarks by Robert Weltsch, still untranslated.

SCHILPP, PAUL A. and FRIEDMAN, MAURICE S., eds. *The Philosophy of Martin Buber*. In my study, the German edition, which preceded the American publication, was used: *Martin Buber* (Stuttgart: W. Kohlhammer, 1963). A Buber symposium, in which Buber answered questions and points of criticism, with contributions by Buber's friend, Ernst Simon, Max Brod, Walter Kaufmann, and others.

WOOD, ROBERT E. *Martin Buber's Ontology. An Analysis of I and Thou* (Evanston: Northwestern University Press, 1969).

Selection of Translated Books of Martin Buber

Pointing the Way. Collected Essays. (New York: Harper & Row, Harper Torchbook, 1963).

I and Thou (New York: Scribner's Sons, 1958).

I and Thou. Martin Buber (New York: Scribner's Sons, 1970).

Tales of Hasidism. 2 vols. (New York: Schocken, 1947).

Images of Good and Evil (New York: Scribner's Sons, 1953).

The Prophetic Faith (New York: Macmillan Co., 1959).

Israel and Palestine (New York: Farrar, Strauss, and Cudahy, 1952).

For the Sake of Heaven, 2nd ed. (New York: Harper and Bros., 1952).

Index